GREEN BAY PACKERS

WHERE HAVE YOU GONE?

PAUL HORNUNG, BRETT FAVRE, JAMES LOFTON, AND OTHER PACKER GREATS

CHUCK CARLSON

SPORTS
PUBLISHING

Sports Publishing books may be purchased in bulk at special discounts for sales promotion, corporate gifts, fund-raising, or educational purposes. Special editions can also be created to specifications. For details, contact the Special Sales Department, Sports Publishing, 307 West 36th Street, 11th Floor, New York, NY 10018 or sportspubbooks@skyhorsepublishing.com.

Sports Publishing® is a registered trademark of Skyhorse Publishing, Inc.®, a Delaware corporation.

Visit our website at www.sportspubbooks.com.

10 9 8 7 6 5 4 3 2 1

Library of Congress Cataloging-in-Publication Data is available on file.

Cover design by Tom Lau
Cover photo credit Associated Press

ISBN: 978-1-61321-811-2
Ebook ISBN: 978-1-61321-855-6

Printed in the United States of America

CONTENTS

ACKNOWLEDGMENTS

It is their inner sanctum, their place of solace and reflection and privacy. No one belongs there unless you belong there. And most don't because those who understand best know you have to earn your way in there and, more to the point, you have to prove you can stay in there by how you perform.

It's the locker room of professional football players and while it may not exactly be sacred, it's at least a place where intruders and interlopers pause before entering.

I know I did. For more than a decade, I poked my nose almost daily into the Green Bay Packers locker room as a sportswriter for the Appleton, Wisconsin, *Post-Crescent* and nearly every day I paused and looked inside, just to see who was there and, yes, who wasn't.

Even on the best of days and in the best of circumstances, it was never a bargain talking to pro football players in their environment.

After all, they had far better things to do with their time than talk to the media and every one of them knew what time we'd be coming in to talk to them about something inane, trivial, or controversial.

So the smart ones made themselves scarce and waited until the media was shuttled out and their locker room belonged only to them again.

But on those days when they were available? It was often gold. Sometimes they would even let their guard down, if only briefly and, if you were lucky, only to you.

All these years later, I still remember talking with the late, great defensive end Reggie White, who spoke as if he were an astronomer discussing the inner workings of the universe when he explained his devastating "club" move, the forearm shiver he developed that turned offensive tackles into mush.

There was the sight of a young quarterback, Brett Favre, walking into the locker room carrying a bag of Gummi-Bears having just signed a very large, very generous contract extension.

Asked about it he simply smiled and said, "It allows me to buy more Gummi-Bears."

Or pensive, unknowable linebacker Wayne Simmons, who discussed his upbringing and future and the meaning of life without knowing he'd die in a fiery car wreck a few years later.

These stories, and so many others, endure because, for just a moment, they offer a peek into the hidden corners of a pro athlete's life and, just as quickly, that door is slammed shut again.

No admittance; nothing to see here; time to move on.

So when I was asked to write this book *Where Have You Gone?* about former Green Bay Packers and what they're up to these days, I figured it would be even more difficult finding these guys. After all, they had no obligations to anyone. The NFL would not fine them for not talking and the team no longer paid their salaries, so they could do what they wanted.

And while I did have my share of issues trying to track down certain players, the task proved less daunting than I had anticipated and for that, I have all those players who talked to me to thank. Most were incredibly gracious as I invaded their privacy one more time—but this time with e-mails, text messages, and phone calls.

They would often ask how much time I'd need for the interview and I would say fifteen, maybe twenty, minutes, and most were happy to give me twice that as they headed off in directions about the past that perhaps they didn't even expect. And I am most appreciative to them for that.

I would also like to thank Katie Hermsen of the Green Bay Packers public relations department who did yeoman duty tracing down players and fielding questions for me. Some decided to participate and some didn't but I appreciated Katie's efforts nonetheless. I'd also like to thank Cliff Christl, the Packers team historian and longtime *Milwaukee Journal Sentinel* sports writer who was also a huge help.

I'd also like to thank Niels Aaboe at Skyhorse Publishing for offering me this opportunity—it was different from a lot of books I've written and came at a time when I didn't think there was anything new for me to learn about this franchise and the guys who played for it. I was wrong. It wasn't an easy project, as I expected, but, then again, nothing worthwhile is.

Finally, I'd like to thank my wife Theresa, who did some impressive copy editing, my sons Patrick and Michael who acted as desperately needed "technical advisors," and my employers at the *Battle Creek Enquirer*, especially executive Michael McCullough, who gave me the latitude and time and support to write.

I hope it's reflected in what you're about to read.

INTRODUCTION

The last question asked was the same for every player: Did you leave the game on your terms?

Some laughed. Some paused, as if still trying to formulate an answer or reconcile in their own heads what had happened when the dream ended.

Some knew it was time. Some left still believing they had plenty to offer to some team willing to provide that opportunity.

Some still wonder what happened all those years later. Some were ready to do something else. Some still can't imagine doing anything else.

Indeed, two players used exactly the same phrase several weeks apart and unsolicited.

"I didn't leave the game, the game left me."

Indeed, it does that to all pro athletes—it's just some are better prepared for it than others.

But they all miss it and that's the common thread. Whether they've been out of football for one year or thirty years, the thrill of the game never leaves them. It's implanted in their DNA and buried in their hearts forever.

Eventually, though, it's the body that makes it clear it's time to leave and they really did know somewhere inside them. They didn't like it, but they knew it. They knew in ways that only an athlete who knows his body so well can know. And they knew that something had changed.

The mind begins to wander during offseason workouts. Recovery time from a game that used to take two days now took five. Suddenly, the wind sprints were a struggle and the moves they used to make so effortlessly two years earlier were just a little harder now.

Time always wins and every athlete knows it, and it's the smart ones who walk away before they're asked to leave.

For others, injury forced the decision to leave the game they loved. Cruel, unexpected and complete, a shattered leg, a wrecked knee, a bad back and that was it.

Former Packers running back Darrell Thompson remembered looking at the X-ray of his ailing hip and realized he could no longer play.

Just like that.

Another Packers running back, the legendary Paul Hornung, realized his longtime neck injury was so bad that if he didn't heed a doctor's warning and retire, he might not walk again.

"Only decision I could make," he said.

Others would try to hook up with other teams, hoping for one more opportunity, hoping to turn time back just a little longer to keep the buzz going and the game alive. But, more often than not, those opportunities only reinforced what everyone else, and the player himself, already knew—it was time to go.

Football is usually not far away for most of them but they have reconciled themselves to the loss.

Some have stayed in football in one way or another—from working as NFL scouts to coaching youth teams. Others have stepped away altogether, unwilling or unable to put the time and energy into a game that they spent so much of their time on.

But they all share the memories of those Sunday afternoons when they were the kings of their universe. Nothing they do now will ever substitute for what they did when they roamed Lambeau Field with, arguably, the NFL's most recognizable franchise and with every Packers fan knowing who they were and what they did. They all found a spot in the Packers firmament and for many of them, they could not have asked for more.

"Greatest time of my life," said offensive guard Marco Rivera.

Where Have You Gone? has sought to find players from all the eras that have made up the remarkable history of the Green Bay Packers franchise.

There are players who played under Vince Lombardi, some of whom bristled at his autocratic methods but realized only later just how much better he made them as players and as men.

There are players who toiled for a Packers franchise in the 1980s that was almost the embodiment of irrelevancy in the rapidly evolving and growing NFL. Indeed, the greatest scare a coach from an NFL team could give to an underperforming player was to threaten to trade them to Green Bay. Don't believe it? More than a few players have said so over the years and, indeed, for this book.

Then something remarkable happened. Team president Bob Harlan decided in 1991 that he'd had enough of the losing and he went out and hired Ron Wolf as general manager, giving the former Oakland Raiders and New York Jets executive the kind of power to reshape the franchise unseen in Green Bay since the days of Lombardi.

His first job was to fire the head coach, Lindy Infante, and bring in Mike Holmgren, a hotshot assistant coach from the San Francisco 49ers. His next job was to wangle a trade with the Atlanta Falcons to bring a young, undisciplined, unruly quarterback to town.

That was Brett Favre.

There are plenty of players in this book from that era too. They are the ones who established a foundation that continues to this day. And many of them still come back to Lambeau Field today to watch the new generation of players who have to find ways to keep that heritage thriving.

Lambeau Field itself has changed a lot. And some teammates are now gone. But the Packers mystique remains.

This book includes some players who were stars and some who were not. They have all moved on to the next phase of their lives. But the game still stays with them, bubbling just below the surface.

And while they're all pursuing different business and personal pursuits now, they all still share the fact that for a brief, glorious time, they were Green Bay Packers and for each of them, it was a time never to be forgotten.

ANTHONY DILWEG

"You never know how close you are to playing."

ANTHONY DILWEG

Position: Quarterback. Ht: 6'3" Wt: 215

Born: March 28, 1965. Packers career: 1989–90

Career Highlights: *Completed 102 of 193 passes for 1,274 yards . . . Named NFC Offensive Player of the Week for September 9, 1990 for 248-yard, three touchdown performance against Rams . . . Third-round draft pick of the Packers in 1988 out of Duke University . . . Grandson of Packers Hall of Famer LaVern Dilweg . . . Wore No. 8.*

Anthony Dilweg was a psychology and drama major at Duke University. He would need to utilize both by the time he was finished with a pro football career that took him from Green Bay to Los Angeles to Montreal to Shreveport, Louisiana and finally out of the game he loved but never really knew.

The psychology? That came as Dilweg fought both his own internal battles and waged external wars to keep playing the game he always knew he could play if given the opportunity.

The drama? That's easy. Dilweg found himself embroiled in quarterback battles in nearly every stop he made.

But through it all—the questions, the doubt, the failure and the injury—he came out the other side smarter and happier and wiser for the experience.

"My last pass was to Sterling [Sharpe] for a touchdown," he said. "At least I can say that."

It was a career that flashed quickly, burned white hot ever so briefly and then flamed out before he even really had a chance to appreciate what was happening. Yet for one week, at the start of the 1990 season, Dilweg was the toast of the NFL and, at least for a little while, was considered perhaps the next great Packers quarterback.

Dilweg had it all—including the size at 6-foot-4, the strong arm, and the smarts that came from playing at Duke under the burgeoning offensive guru Steve Spurrier.

He even had the Packers pedigree since he was the grandson of LaVern Dilweg, who had played for the Packers from 1927–34 and was considered perhaps the best offensive end in the NFL before future Hall of Famer, and teammate, Don Hutson arrived on the scene.

So it seemed like a great match when Dilweg was selected by the Packers in the third round of that infamous 1989 draft. Indeed, Dilweg was considered little more than an afterthought in that draft after Green Bay selected Michigan State tackle Tony Mandarich with the second overall pick, bypassing future Hall of Famers Barry Sanders, Derrick Thomas, Troy Aikman, and Deion Sanders.

"I was certainly very honored to be drafted by the Packers," Dilweg said, "I didn't think I would be drafted by them because we hadn't talked that much before the draft. But I was prepared to compete."

And there would be an opportunity since the Packers weren't exactly flush with quarterback talent. Don Majkowski had gained most of the starts and split time with Randy Wright in 1988. But neither player accomplished much as the Packers staggered to a 4–12 record, their 10th straight non-winning season.

So in 1989, second-year coach Lindy Infante decided to give the starting job to the flamboyant, talented but often erratic Majkowski and Dilweg would back him up.

Dilweg accepted it but didn't necessarily agree.

"My rookie year, I thought I could compete for the starting job," he said.

But that chance never came.

What he saw from the sidelines was a season for the ages. Behind Majkowski, who would earn the nickname "The Majic Man," the Packers posted four one-point wins, still an NFL record, and rally to win six games in dramatic, late-game fashion.

There was Majkowski, his blonde locks flowing from under his helmet, completing one impossible pass after another and leading the Packers to another improbable victory that earned the team another nickname, "The Cardiac Pack." Majkowski threw for more than 4,300 yards and 27 touchdowns as Green Bay posted a 10–6 record, its highest total since 1972.

And though they missed the playoffs due to a tiebreaker with the Minnesota Vikings, fans were giddy as they viewed a bright, glorious future under their new star quarterback and the master motivator, Infante. Indeed, in an offseason poll by the *Milwaukee Journal*, Infante was voted the best coach in Packers history, beating out some guy named Lombardi.

Dilweg saw it all and began to wonder what his future in Green Bay might be. And even now he recalls a game early in the 1989 season he thought could have changed his future with the team.

It was September 24 and the Packers, who had rallied from a 24–7 halftime deficit the week before to beat the New Orleans Saints, were trailing the Los Angeles Rams 38–7 at halftime in Anaheim, California.

"Lindy told me he was going to Don one more series in the third quarter against the Rams and if he couldn't do anything, he was going to put me in," Dilweg said. "You never know how close you are to playing."

As it turned out Majkowski led the Packers to an opening touchdown drive and he stayed in and nearly pulled out another miracle win.

Dilweg ended up only throwing one pass that season.

But the winds shifted that offseason. The Packers' success from the 1989 season led several key players, including Majkowski, to seek renegotiated contracts. Majkowski was seeking a new deal worth $3 million a season and the Packers offered $1.2 million.

The holdout eventually grew protracted and nasty but into the vacuum stepped Dilweg, knowing all he could do was perform the best he could and let the situation take care of itself.

"I was really excited to get the opportunity," he said.

And he knew if he could play well in the preseason, it would solidify his position as a starter, but he also knew it might also spur Majkowski to get back to camp.

"It was a little dicey in the preseason," he said. "I played OK against Cleveland then I played badly against Kansas City. I struggled a bit. They signed Don that week."

Indeed, the Packers and Majkowski agreed on a one-year deal worth $1.5 million and incentives that could earn him $2 million a season.

But he had missed forty-five days of camp and all four pre-season games and was in no position to start the season opener against the Rams.

"I was hoping Don would hold out all season," Dilweg said with a laugh. "But I was a little naïve. He had a great relationship with the offensive line. I knew I was on borrowed time because there was a Pro Bowler coming up behind me. But I didn't have anxiety about having bad game, a bad quarter. I was just excited for the opportunity."

Dilweg started slowly in that season-opener, hurting his right thumb when his hand collided with a teammate's helmet.

"Lindy said, 'That's OK, I've got Don,'" Dilweg recalled, spurring him to a competitive level he wasn't sure he even had. "I said, 'I'm fine.' They were going to have to take me off on a stretcher."

Dilweg would go on to complete 20 of 32 passes for 248 yards and three touchdowns as the Packers posted a 36–24 win. He was named NFC Offensive Player of the Week and whispers began of an honest-to-God quarterback controversy in Green Bay.

Dilweg was exuberant about his performance but it didn't last long.

"I was so excited when I saw the film the next day," he said. "But Lindy said, 'You could have had six touchdown passes that game.' I was half depressed after that. I still see [tight end] Jackie Harris in the back of the end zone on a pass that I missed and I realized that game wasn't as great as I thought it was."

It also got Dilweg thinking about his place as a quarterback in the NFL.

"I really hadn't played a lot of quarterback," he said. "I played one year in high school and one year in college and I felt I had so much to prove."

It was especially true when he thought of his relationship with Majkowski, who was on the other end of the spectrum from the quieter, more cerebral Dilweg. Majkowski blossomed in the spotlight in the 1989 season, when he directed so many late-game rallies, fueling his belief that the Packers were his team And he may have been correct.

But Dilweg remembers after his season-opening performance against the Rams that Majkowski was gracious and supportive.

"Don was great," he said. "He's a competitor too. But after the game he came up to me and was like 'Wow.' But I think deep down he knew he was ready to take over again. Quarterback relationships are complicated. It's always a deep-seated competition. You want that guy's job."

Dilweg admits he and Majkowski were never great friends and he was closer to No. 3 quarterback Blair Kiel.

"It was really competitive," he said.

Dilweg and Majkowski split practice time with the first-team offense that next week but Dilweg got the start against the Chicago Bears.

"I felt a little relieved when I heard that. I prepared hard."

But the results weren't pretty. In fact, as great as Dilweg played the week before in front of the home folks, he probably could not have been worse against the rival Bears at Lambeau Field.

Dilweg completed just 14 of 28 passes for 148 yards and one interception. He was sacked six times and finally gave way to Majkowski in the fourth quarter. But it didn't matter, the Packers were overwhelmed, 31–13.

"I felt beat up after that game," Dilweg recalled. "I remember Lindy apologized to me for having to put up with all that. It was so bad I remember that [guard] Rich Moran said to me in the huddle, 'Why don't you throw another interception and really piss [the fans] off?' It wasn't fun."

Majkowski got the start the next week against the Kansas City Chiefs and kept it, helping lead the Packers back to respectability.

Then Majkowski was lost for the season with a shoulder injury against the Phoenix Cardinals. Dilweg returned to the lineup, led the Packers to a win in that game and again the following week against the Tampa Bay Buccaneers, and the Packers were 6–5 and right back in the playoff chase.

"We started feeling like it was 1989 all over again," Dilweg said. "Then we hit the five-game wall."

That was Green Bay's last win of the season and Dilweg would find himself in and out of the lineup the rest of the season, due in part to inconsistency and in part to injury.

Against the Seattle Seahawks, Dilweg was awful, completing just 6 of 22 passes for 69 yards and one interception and was replaced by Blair Kiel, who nearly rallied the Packers back to victory.

"I laid an egg," Dilweg said simply.

Against the Philadelphia Eagles, a disastrous 31–0 loss, Dilweg suffered a collapsed foot arch when Mandarich stepped on it. That added to the ruptured bursa sac in his elbow.

The season finally ended with a loss to the Vikings in which Dilweg did not play badly—throwing for 232 yards and a fourth quarter touchdown to Sterling Sharpe.

"I did not want to end the season not playing that game," he said.

But his season ended ignominiously when a snap near his own end zone went over his head.

"My career ended on a safety," he said with a laugh.

Dilweg would never play another NFL game and, he admits now, the thought of walking was already occurring to him.

"I remember thinking I'm 6'3 ½" with skinny legs," he said. "I've got a good education and there are things I want to do after football. This is tough."

As the 1991 season dawned, Infante made the decision to keep Majkowski, Kiel, and veteran Mike Tomczak at quarterback. But Dilweg was unconcerned.

"I thought I'd be picked up pretty quickly," he said.

He had opportunities with the Cardinals and he had a tryout for San Francisco 49ers quarterback coach Mike Holmgren, who showed interest in signing him if Steve Young's back injury didn't allow him to play anymore. The call never came.

"I got a chip on my shoulder," Dilweg said. "The more teams didn't sign me the more pissed off I got. I was determined I'd get back."

He met with Raiders owner Al Davis seeking a chance to just show what he could do and Davis told him, "The verdict on you is the glass is either half full or half empty."

So desperate to get a chance, Dilweg hired a plane to fly over Raiders practice with the message "Mr. Davis—Give me a chance" and "Quarterback for Hire."

"And at that point I had nothing to lose," he said.

And while he signed with the Raiders in 1991, he never got through preseason.

He hooked up with the Montreal Machine of the World Football League in 1992 and then the Shreveport Pirates of the Canadian Football League, but the injuries began to pile up.

Still, through it all, Dilweg didn't want to give up.

"It doesn't die easily," he said. "It's in your system."

Since his rookie season, Dilweg had developed an interest in real estate as an investment and in 1993, he got his commercial real estate license and in 1999 started his own real estate company in Durham, North Carolina, the Dilweg Companies.

His company now has a half billion dollars in assets, Dilweg said, and it's become one of the top real estate companies in the region.

"I've always enjoyed business-centric things," he said. "I started from the ground up. My greatest business experience was football. I love my guys and I love being in the trenches with them. We have a little over thirty employees and we're in the middle of a growth—we're expanding to Atlanta, Charlotte, and Raleigh-Durham. I enjoy what I do."

But football is never far away.

He coaches his two daughters' soccer team as well as his son's football team. His boy plays linebacker and, of course, quarterback.

He said his days in Green Bay may not have gone as he had hoped, but he wouldn't trade them for anything.

"I really enjoyed the community and the people," he said. "It was more like a college football environment. It was painful making the transition out of football and I would have loved to have played more. But look at all the stuff I learned. I had two knee reconstructions but I'd do it all over again and I'm grateful for the experience."

BARTY SMITH

"I have never lived in the rear-view mirror."

BARTY SMITH

Position: Fullback. Ht: 6'3" Wt: 250

Born: March 23, 1952. Packers career: 1974–80

Career Highlights: First-round draft pick of the Packers in 1974 out of the University of Richmond . . . Rushed for 1,942 yards and scored 18 touchdowns and caught 120 passes in his Packers career . . . Named Packers' Offensive Player of the Year in 1977 . . . Wore No. 33.

Life is good for Barty Smith. Sure the knees, the subject of ten surgeries including two replacements, continue to plague him, and the shoulders, which required two surgeries, bother him, and the elbows, which needed three operations, ache, and the back is sore.

But the former first-round draft pick whose promising career almost ended before it started has no regrets. He lives in his hometown of Richmond, Virginia, still his favorite place on earth, doing a job he loves. He has family and friends and memories to last a lifetime and his Packers experience, despite the pain of injuries and the fact he played for some pretty bad teams, remains a source of joy.

"My problems are strictly physical and I can live with them," he said. "I wouldn't have missed the experience for anything in the world. I always felt I could be a little stronger, a little tougher than the guy across from me and that's what I always tried to do. But pro football is a profession very few people say they'd love to do. I loved it."

For more than thirty years, Smith has worked at Loveland Distributors in Richmond, where his company sells beer, wine, and liquor throughout the region.

"I've only had two jobs in my life," he said. "I guess I've been blessed."

That first job, of course, was football. At the University of Richmond, he was one of those rare combinations of size and speed. He was a great runner who could also catch the ball out of the backfield, a skill that was coming into growing importance in the NFL. Perhaps his greatest skill, though, was as a blocker. In fact, he was named college football's top blocking football player in both 1973 and 1974.

So he was on the radar of several NFL teams in the 1974 draft—one was the Green Bay Packers, a franchise with a great past, and the other was the Dallas Cowboys, a franchise with a bright future.

"I'd been talking to representatives from both Green Bay and Dallas before the draft and the guy from the Cowboys said they were going to take me with the 23rd pick if I was still there," Smith said.

He wasn't.

The Packers instead grabbed him with the 12th pick, envisioning him as the guy who would open holes for rising star tailback John Brockington and provide a spark in the backfield.

But it was not to be.

Even today, Smith can remember the circumstances behind a devastating knee injury that likely changed his career.

It's hard to imagine a circumstance like this in today's NFL, where every player is a multi-million dollar commodity not to be placed in harm's way of any kind.

But back then, many college players took part in late summer all-star games, in many cases after having already signed with the NFL team that had drafted them.

One of the cases was Smith, who had signed with the Packers and then played in the Coaches All-Star Game in Lubbock, Texas, on a blistering August night.

"I was having a huge game," Smith recalled. "I rushed for something like 85 yards in the first half. I was on a roll."

But Smith also recalled the field was artificial turf and the temperature on that field had spiked to 110 degrees.

In the third quarter, Smith continued his strong play, bursting through the line for a big gain. At the end of the run, he planted his foot just as a defender came up to hit him.

"The defensive back's name was Ozell Collier from Colorado," said Smith. "I don't know whatever happened to him."

Collier collided with Smith's planted left leg, shattering Smith's knee and tearing just about every ligament that could be torn.

"I got up and I knew it didn't feel right," he said. "I went back to the huddle and I put my hands on my knees like I always did and my knee just collapsed."

He had torn his medial collateral and anterior cruciate ligaments, among other things, an injury that today would require a year to recover from. But Smith didn't have that kind of time.

He felt he was under pressure to perform because of his status as a No. 1 draft pick and he tried to rush back to the field.

Indeed, standing on the sidelines watching practices and games was the worst feeling he had ever known.

"I felt like a total outsider," he said. "I was so depressed. I couldn't do a thing and I felt like a schmuck. It was a bad time in my life."

So Smith battled his way back before he was physically ready.

"I was back practicing in late September, early October," he said. "I came back too early, there's no question about that."

And he knew almost immediately something was different.

"Before the injury, I had always run a consistent 4.6 [40-yard dash] and I was 250 pounds," he said. "That was pretty good. But after the injury, I never got below 4.8. I didn't understand I was coming back too early."

Smith did get back on the field eventually and proved to be a solid contributor to a Packers team that was going nowhere fast.

In 1975, former Packers great quarterback Bart Starr took over from Dan Devine as head coach, but Smith is convinced Starr never had a chance.

"Dan had stacked the deck against Bart because of that trade," Smith said.

"That trade," as any longtime Packers fan knows, was the one engineered by Devine in October 1974 when he wrecked the Packers future by sending two first-round draft choices, two second-rounders and a third-round pick to the Los Angeles Rams for a thirty-four-year-old quarterback, John Hadl, whose best years were far behind him. Hadl started 19 games over two seasons and threw nine touchdown passes and 29 interceptions.

The result—for Starr, for the Packers and for Smith—was almost unrelenting misery on the field.

The Packers were 4–10 in 1975, 5–9 in 1976, and 4–10 in 1977. In 1978, there was a glimmer of hope as the Packers started the season 6–1, but they fell apart and finished 8–7–1.

"I admired Bart immensely," Smith said. "Every team meeting was like the best sales meeting I'd ever been in. I think he eventually could have turned it around."

Meanwhile, Smith soldiered on with a bad knee that was never going to get any better. Nonetheless, he was named the Packers Offensive Player of the Year in 1977, something of a dubious distinction in a season when the Packers scored just 134 points in 14 games.

"It was a nice honor," said Smith, who ran for 554 yards and two touchdowns and caught 37 passes for 340 yards and another score. "But come on, I caught 37 passes. Whoopee. We were just not very good."

That was Smith's high point with the Packers. Another running back, Terdell Middleton, was brought in and Smith went back to his role as primarily a blocking back.

By the start of the 1980 season, Smith knew it was time to walk away while he still could walk away.

"I had fluid on my knee all the time," he said. "It got progressively worse. I remember working out prior to my sixth and seventh seasons and I was in tears afterward. It was a tough road. I probably hung on two years longer than I should have but I loved the game so much."

He finally retired in 1980, in a very real sense from the injury he had suffered on that hot August night six years earlier in Texas.

As for what might have been with the Cowboys?

"If I would've been selected by Dallas, I'd be looking at a Super Bowl ring now," he said. "But I truly don't think about it. The caliber of people I met in Green Bay was incredible. I loved those people. They embraced me even when I was hurt and I'll never forget that. And we weren't even winners and they still embraced us. It was an honor to play for them."

After the NFL, Smith decided to look for the second job he'd ever had and focused on opening a restaurant.

"I had a group of investors and the more I looked around, the more people told me to stay away from restaurants," he said. "There was a high mortality rate and I was a little green then. But I was still interested in the industry because I like meeting people, I like talking to people."

So he signed up with Loveland, a Richmond company in the third generation with the same family. He's now the senior vice president and general manager and remains as happy now as he was when he started.

"I love my management team," he said. "I am a planner. I don't like loose ends. My whole life has been like that. There have been a few turns but the good Lord has kept me on track."

Well-known in Richmond for the work he's done there over the years, his exploits with the Packers still resonate with a lot of people and he's happy to relive a time that remains special to him.

"It's amazing to me," he said. "I get cards from people all the time. I have boxes overflowing from people thanking me for playing and people around here bring it up all the time. It was a tough way to earn a living but I had a great time."

JOHN DORSEY

"I take no day for granted."

JOHN DORSEY

Position: Linebacker. Ht: 6'2" Wt: 240

Born: August 30, 1960. Packers career: 1984–89

Career Highlights: Fourth-round draft pick of the Packers from the University Connecticut . . . His 35 special teams tackles in 1984 is a team record . . . Recorded 130 career tackles . . . Went on to serve in Packers scouting department for twenty-one years . . . Wore No. 99.

John Dorsey has never forgotten where he came from or how he got to where he is. How could he? Every experience in his life and every place he's been has formed a key part of the man who has reached the pinnacle of the National Football League.

These days, he's general manager of the Kansas City Chiefs, a position he has keenly and thoroughly trained for but which still causes him to shake his head in amazement at where he's come from and how he got there.

John Dorsey wraps up Phil McConkey during a pre-season game in 1985. (AP Photo/Ron Frehm)

"I've seen everything," he said. "I've seen the good, I've seen the bad. I've seen it all."

But to understand who John Dorsey is now, it's crucial to understand who he was and how he got here.

He grew up in a little town called Leonardtown, Maryland, located on a strip of land between several bodies of water in Southern Maryland, a place famous for its blue crabs and oysters and slowpitch softball.

His family name goes back to the Revolution in that area and his dad, Walter, was a state senator and the county's longtime state's attorney. This place forged the person John Dorsey would become.

He was star football player at Fork Union Academy High School and went on to play football at the University of Connecticut, where he was a four-year star at linebacker. In 1984, he was a fourth-round draft pick of the Green Bay Packers and that would begin a nearly three-decade stint with the franchise.

He was never a star player with the Packers but he was a special teams standout and a smart, driven player who soon developed a reputation as a guy who maximized every bit of potential he had. Indeed, his 35 special teams tackles in 1984 is still a team record. In his five years as a player, he finished with 130 tackles from his linebacker spot.

"Since I started playing, I only focused on being the best player I could be," he said. "I knew I wasn't the best and as soon as I started giving second best, I'd be left by the wayside."

And perhaps no one appreciated his time in the NFL as much as John Dorsey, whose career was cut short in 1989 when, incredibly, he injured his knee during a pre-game warm-up in the season opener.

He was placed on injured reserve, did not play that season and soon grew to realize that his days as a player were coming to an end.

"Even on that last day as a player, I pinched myself," he said. "I never thought I'd get six years in the NFL. It was just a joy."

And it seems every minute that he's been involved with the NFL has been recorded in a Dorsey memory bank.

"I remember sitting down and signing my first contract," he said. "It was the greatest six years of my life in football. I love that town and that organization."

Indeed, even though he's now running a rival organization, Dorsey still keeps the same Green Bay cell phone number he's had for years.

"Why change?" he said. "That's how everybody can reach me."

Instead of cursing his bad luck as he saw his playing career end, Dorsey saw it as an opportunity to move to the next phase of his career.

That began innocuously enough when Dorsey was trying to rehab his knee injury but was beginning to realize, as every player eventually does, that the end might be looming.

"It didn't dawn on me to move into the front office," he said. "That last year I was hurt and I knew I wasn't the same player I had been."

He then had a chance conversation with team president Bob Harlan, who asked if he wanted to join the team's scouting department. In 1991, he was hired by Packers vice president of football operations Tom Braatz to scout linebackers.

But it seemed Dorsey's new career might meet a quick ending when, after the Packers disastrous 1991 season, Braatz was fired. Harlan then hired Ron Wolf, who was brought in as general manager with orders to fix the sputtering franchise in any way he saw necessary.

"I was scouting in New Jersey when Ron Wolf called me," Dorsey recalled. "He asked me if I could run the computer system and I said I could."

That began a relationship that continued for years and, really, continues even today even though Wolf has been retired for years and Dorsey has moved on.

"I was too young and naïve to think about anything else," Dorsey said. "I put my head down and went to work."

And for the next two decades, Dorsey learned at the knee of one of the NFL's top personnel evaluators. Part luck, part coincidence but mostly through the kind of hard work Dorsey has come to exemplify, he became part of one of the NFL's premier scouting departments.

"If you want to aspire to be a winning organization, you have to work hard to do it," he said. "My best record in six years as a player was 8–8 and some guys thought they'd won the Super Bowl. I couldn't understand that."

It was the influence of his mentor, Ron Wolf, and head coach Mike Holmgren, both of whom had come from winning, committed organizations, that showed Dorsey something in Green Bay really was changing.

"They told all of us we're there to win championships and there are going to have to be sacrifices," he said. "I thought that was refreshing."

Dorsey began his tenure with the Packers as a relentless scout, who would go everywhere and anywhere he needed to go to find the players that would make the Packers a better team.

And in that time, he and Wolf grew close.

"He used to drive around town and that's where he'd have his meeting," Dorsey recalled. "That was always a big deal. He'd say, 'Let's go for a drive.' We'd get a lot of stuff figured out in those drives."

It began to pay dividends in 1995 when the Packers went to San Francisco and upset the powerful 49ers in the NFC playoffs, earning a spot in the NFC title game where they were beaten by the stronger, faster, more experienced Dallas Cowboys.

But the template had been created and the Packers knew they were close to being a team that could not only get back to the title game but win it and return to the Super Bowl.

That happened the next year when the Packers, in front of a raucous Lambeau Field crowd, beat the Carolina Panthers, earning them their first trip to the Super Bowl in thirty years. For Dorsey, in many ways it was that performance that meant more than the actual Super Bowl because he had recommended and scouted many of the players who made up that roster.

"In your little way, you knew you were part of doing something special," Dorsey said. "Very satisfying. It was a moment of pride."

Barely three weeks after the Packers won Super Bowl XXXII in New Orleans they acknowledged Dorsey's contributions and talent by promoting him to director of college scouting.

The next year the Packers went back to the Super Bowl with a team that Wolf thought was even better than the one that had won it all the year before. But the Packers fell to the Denver Broncos and cracks in the team foundation were starting to show.

Holmgren, who had been head coach for seven years, was growing restless and wanted to add general manager to his title. But Wolf was entrenched and had no plans to go anywhere anytime soon. Holmgren coached one more season in Green Bay, which ended with a devastating last-second playoff loss to the 49ers.

Barely a week later, he was named head coach and general manager of the Seattle Seahawks and he brought Dorsey with him, making him director of player personnel. He stayed there a year but the lure of Green Bay was too strong and he returned to the Packers a year later. In February 2001 Wolf retired as Packers general manager and coach Mike Sherman assumed the role.

For Dorsey, it was the end of an era, both for the team he worked for and personally.

"Ron is a very humble man," Dorsey said. "He deeply cares about football and the Green Bay Packers—even now. What I love is his respect for the game. He'd always say, 'Where would you rather be than Green Bay, Wisconsin?' He was always so meticulous and he taught me so much. At a young age, I was trying to accumulate as much knowledge as I could and he helped me do that. If you want to learn everything, he'll teach you everything."

So few people were happier than Dorsey in February 2015 when Wolf was elected to the Pro Football Hall of Fame in Canton, Ohio.

Dorsey remained in his role as director of college scouting where he again helped lead the Packers to a Super Bowl title in 2010. In 2012 he was promoted to director of football operations, working hand in hand with general manager Ted Thompson.

For Dorsey, the journey continued when in January 2013, he was named general manager of the Kansas City Chiefs, a franchise seeking a new start after a disastrous 2–14 season the year before.

Ironically, the week before, the Chiefs hired a longtime Dorsey friend, Andy Reid, as head coach. Reid had served as tight ends coach and quarterbacks coach in Green Bay before he was named head coach of the Philadelphia Eagles. But after fourteen years with the Eagles, Reid had been fired.

Together, the old Green Bay duo helped orchestrate one of the great turnarounds in NFL history as the Chiefs posted an 11–5 record and reached the playoffs. For his efforts, Dorsey was named Executive of the Year by the Pro Football Writers Association of America.

John Dorsey has come a long way from the days as a special teams demon for a moribund Green Bay Packers franchise in the mid 1980s.

He has watched a franchise grow and change and become, in many ways, the gold standard of how NFL franchises should be run. And all he wants to do is live by the principles he was taught by so many people over the years.

"I've been blessed to be around some of the best people in football," he said. "The key is to be true to your own self. You roll up your sleeves and go to work. Always tell the truth and realize there are no shortcuts because this is a hard business. And I learned long ago that you take no day for granted."

ADAM TIMMERMAN

"It was a neat time to be there."

ADAM TIMMERMAN

Position: Offensive guard. Ht: 6'4" Wt: 310

Born: August 14, 1971. Packers career: 1995–98

Career Highlights: *Seventh-round draft pick of the Packers in 1995 from South Dakota State. . . . Started 48 of 61 games for Packers, including two Super Bowls . . . Wore No. 63.*

Y ou can go home again. Of course, Adam Timmerman didn't know there was an alternative.

He grew up in a little place called Cherokee, Iowa, a classic Midwestern farm community in northwest Iowa that is almost equidistant between Sioux Falls, South Dakota and Sioux City, Iowa.

It's a community of 5,000 people buried deep in the cornfields and where agriculture remains not only a way of life, but a necessity. And it's where Timmerman grew up, became a star athlete at Washington High School and, eventually, after twelve

Adam Timmerman gives Frank Winters (52) a boost after a Packers score in Super Bowl XXXI. (AP Photo/Susan Sterner)

years in the NFL trenches, it's where he happily moved back to with his family once his career ended.

"My wife [Jana] and I were born in Cherokee," Timmerman said. "My kids [Mason, Alexa, and Jada] enjoy the school system. My mom still lives here. This is home."

Indeed, it's where he always came back to after another rugged NFL season, the place where he could relax, rejuvenate and reflect on a career that he never could have imagined all those years ago. In his career, Timmerman played his first four seasons with the Green Bay Packers, going to two Super Bowls, and the next eight with the St. Louis Rams, where he played in two more Super Bowls. He has two championship rings and was part of two teams playing at the pinnacle of their powers.

"Timing is everything," Timmerman said. "I was on good teams and in good organizations with good coaches. And both organizations, the leadership on both of them was great. I couldn't have asked for more."

There wasn't much of a ripple in the 1995 draft when the Packers selected Timmerman, an intriguing if unknown offensive guard from South Dakota State, with a seventh-round pick, Green Bay's last pick of the draft.

Seventh-round selections usually had the job security of South American dictators and this seemed especially the case for a Packers organization that looked to be building into something special.

In 1994, Green Bay had reached the playoffs for the first time in twelve years.

They had a great young quarterback in Brett Favre, they had a major free-agent signing in defensive end Reggie White and they had a coach in Mike Holmgren and a general manager in Ron Wolf who seemed single-minded in their plans for the future.

This was a team headed somewhere in a hurry and into this stepped a decidedly overwhelmed Timmerman.

"My eyes were wide open when I got to Green Bay," he said. "At South Dakota State, it was three years before I got my first new pair of shoes. And then I get to Green Bay and I saw Brett Favre throw his first pass and I said, 'Yep, we're not in South Dakota anymore.'"

But what no one knew at the time was just how successful the Packers '95 draft would prove to be.

Craig Newsome was the first-round pick and would step in as a starting cornerback and stay for several years. In the third round, the Packers had four selections—defensive tackle Darius Holland, fullback William Henderson, linebacker Brian Williams, and wide receiver Antonio Freeman. All would end up as starters while Freeman, Henderson, and Williams would eventually earn All-Pro honors.

The Packers also got a special teams star in running back Travis Jervey in the fifth round and Timmerman in the seventh, who would battle his way into the starting lineup midway into his rookie season and never let it go.

"I remember reading how terrible everyone thought the '95 draft class was," he said. "We were offended."

"I remember Mike Holmgren told us early in camp not to count the players at your position," Timmerman recalled. "He said, 'Make it hard for us to cut you.'"

Timmerman did just that, latching on to an offensive line full of veterans like Frank Winters, Aaron Taylor, and Ken Ruettgers.

"I felt I was very blessed to have had an offensive line coach like Tom Lovat," he said. "He really worked with me. And Frankie and Harry Galbreath, they were veteran players who brought me along pretty fast."

Timmerman was inactive his first three games and then was thrust into a starting role in week four when guard Taylor suffered a season-ending knee injury.

Never flashy, he took his role seriously but with the appreciation of a seventh-round draft pick who never really knew from one week to the next if he still had a job.

But Timmerman's steady, solid play at left guard was exactly what the Packers needed and he would go on to start 55 consecutive games from 1996–98, including two Super Bowls.

For a small-town Iowa kid, starting in Super Bowls in New Orleans and San Diego for the Green Bay Packers wasn't even a dream come true because he'd never even had such dreams.

Still, he believes the best Packers team he played for didn't even reach the Super Bowl.

"I thought the 1995 team was better than either one of the Super Bowl teams," he said. "We had everything."

That was the team that went to San Francisco and upset the 49ers in the second round of the playoffs and then went to Dallas and fell to the eventual Super Bowl champion Cowboys, despite outplaying them the first three quarters. It was also when Holmgren stood up in the plane on the trip back to Green Bay and told his players to remember how this felt and to never let it happen again.

But as Timmerman kept proving himself week in and week out, he never got the feeling the Packers were comfortable with his play.

"I think they drafted every year to replace me," he said with a laugh. "I don't think I ever got comfortable."

Indeed, in 1997 the Packers did draft John Michels, an offensive tackle, with their first-round pick and Marco Rivera with their sixth-round pick, and Ross Verba, a guard, with their first pick in 1998. But Timmerman could never be unseated.

He had hoped that consistency and quality would count for something when he became a free agent prior to the 1999 season.

"I didn't want to go," he said. "My wife and I both loved Green Bay. It was the perfect situation. We met a lot of great people and I remember how near and dear we were to the people. We still have a lot of good friends there. It was a neat time to be there."

But above all, the NFL is a business and Timmerman was seeking a new contract that the Packers didn't think they could meet.

"When Green Bay didn't offer me a contract, it made the decision easier," he said.

Timmerman viewed the Philadelphia Eagles, where former Packers line coach Andy Reid was now the new head coach, and the St. Louis Rams as his best options in free agency.

"I loved Andy and I wanted to play for him," Timmerman said. "But I really hit it off with [Rams' coach] Dick Vermeil and [line coach] Jim Hanifan and it came down to staying in the Midwest. I told Andy that and he said, 'I can't believe that's the criteria you're using.'"

But home is a strong draw, especially for someone like Timmerman. Besides, he found himself right back in the middle of a franchise that was on the verge of something special, just as the Packers had been when he arrived.

His first season in St. Louis, he was part of the Rams high-flying offense nicknamed the "Greatest Show on Turf" that went on to post a 13–3 regular season and beat the Tennessee Titans in Super Bowl XXXIV.

Two years later, the Rams were back in the Super Bowl with a team that might have been even better than the championship team. But the Rams were beaten in the final seconds by the New England Patriots.

Nonetheless, in the course of a seven-year career to date, Timmerman had started in four Super Bowls, winning two of them.

"The funny thing is I remember more from the two losses than I did from the two wins," he said. "That's kind of sad."

Timmerman would not miss a start in eight seasons with the Rams but he also knew that time was drawing short on his career. In his eight seasons with the Rams, he was voted a Pro Bowl alternate from 1999 to 2002 and actually played in the showcase twice.

"I remember Dick Vermeil told me that time flies in this game—when you're winning," he said,

The Rams did make two more playoff appearances in 2003 and 2004 but their time had come and gone and so, too, had Timmerman's. He was released February 27, 2007 and retired soon after.

"It flew by," Timmerman said of his career where he played in 187 games and started 172.

But for him, home awaited.

"I was always interested in farming and agriculture," he said.

So the family returned to Cherokee where the roots run deep, as they always have.

Timmerman didn't miss a step, returning to what he grew up with and loved most.

"I always wanted to farm with my dad," Timmerman said.

But that dream ended when his dad Larry, was killed in an ATV accident in 1999. Still he never lost his love of the land and in 2004 he purchased ICON Ag and Turf, with several locations throughout northwestern Iowa, servicing and selling John Deere farm equipment.

He's the general manager and runs the store in LeMars, which is just forty miles from their home in Cherokee.

"I was always interested in farming and agriculture so it's all worked out," he said.

Not bad for a small-town Iowan from a small school who started his NFL career in the league's smallest city. Through the 2014 season, he remains the only player in league history to have won one Super Bowl and lost a second with two different teams and he wouldn't trade the experience.

Timmerman has returned to Green Bay every year since his retirement to watch a game and recapture a time that will remain special to him.

"They do a good job of taking care of former players," he said. "And that's got to be a hard thing to do with the list of alumni that franchise has had. And I was just happy to be a part of it."

DARRELL THOMPSON

"There's nothing like it."

DARRELL THOMPSON

Position: Running back. Ht: 6'0" Wt: 215

Born: November 23, 1967. Packers career: 1990–94

Career Highlights: *First-round draft pick of the Packers out of the University of Minnesota . . . Rushed for 1,641 yards and seven touchdowns in five seasons . . . Caught 41 passes for 333 yards and one score . . . Wore No. 39.*

They never tell what it's like to be a first-round draft pick in the National Football League. Darrell Thompson thought he had some idea but, in the end, he really didn't. Nobody knows because only a handful of players ever get to be in that position.

And for Thompson, a running back from the University of Minnesota, the feeling was uncertainty and anxiety and anticipation and everything in between.

"You have to remember, these were in the days before cell phones," Thompson said. "I joke that the team that drafts you doesn't talk to you very much before the draft. I had heard from others but not really from the Packers. But I remember I connected with running backs coach Willie Peete and we really got along."

Thompson admits he felt pressure as one of two first-round draft picks the Packers had in 1990. University of Mississippi linebacker Tony Bennett was taken by the Packers with the 18th pick in the first round and, on the very next selection, they grabbed Thompson.

It was a nod to the fact that the Packers needed help on both sides of the ball, despite coming off a raucous, exciting, bizarre 1989 season that saw the Packers rally time and again for close wins, end up with a 10–6 record and still miss the playoffs.

Bennett was a big, fast athletic linebacker and Thompson's numbers at Minnesota were gaudy and impressive.

He remains the only Minnesota running back to rush for more than 4,000 career yards. He also ran for 40 touchdowns, posted 23 100-yard rushing games in four seasons and ended up with 5,109 all-purpose yards.

Thompson was being hailed by college football writers across the country as one of the best-kept secrets in the game—a versatile, tough runner who could run and catch passes and make any offense better.

And that wasn't lost on the Packers either, who felt they were just a player or two away from returning to NFL respectability.

In the mind of Tom Braatz, the Packers vice president of football operations, and head coach Lindy Infante, he would be the ideal complement to quarterback Don Majkowski, who was coming off an All-Pro season where he threw for more than 4,000 yards.

But it never quite worked out—that season or, frankly, any of the five he played for the Packers.

"I remember watching D.J. Dozier play for the Minnesota Vikings and I didn't think he felt very good about what he was being asked to do," Thompson said. "I didn't understand being put in a situation where you couldn't do what you knew you could do best. They asked him to run sideways and that wasn't his strength. Lo and behold, that's what the Packers asked me to do."

And it would prove to be an issue for several years.

That first season, Thompson rushed just 76 times for only 264 yards and scored one touchdown. He also caught just three passes, for one yard, all season. His best performance, ironically, came in the last game of the season when he rushed for 63 yards on just six carries in a loss to the Broncos that ended the Packers disastrous season at 6–10.

Thompson, who had known nothing but success in his football career, was shaken and confused after that first year.

"I did wonder what was going on," he said. "It's impossible for a college guy to understand the NFL. There's nothing like it."

His second season didn't start off appreciably better. It was clear to players and fans alike that the magic of 1989 was long gone and as the 1991 season progressed, the Packers offense was going nowhere fast. Majkowski struggled with inconsistency and injury and the Packers could not find a reliable option at running back, including Thompson. The Packers eventually used three quarterbacks that season—Majkowski, Mike Tomczak, and Blair Kiel—and a host of running backs but nothing worked.

The Packers staggered to a 4–12 record, costing both Infante and Braatz their jobs. And Thompson, who was the team's leading rusher that season with 471 yards, was wondering if an NFL career was really for him.

"We had so many off-the-field issues," said Thompson, who to this day remains a fan of Lindy Infante and the job he tried to do under what proved to be almost impossible circumstances. "Smart coaches put you in a position to be successful."

That's what Thompson hoped would happen when Mike Holmgren, the offensive whiz who had helped construct the San Francisco 49ers potent offense, came to Green Bay as head coach in 1992.

"I did see changes," Thompson said. "He made things simpler and he made us more students of the game. He gave smaller bites and made sure we did them well. He made us understand why our practice mattered. He was precise but Lindy was precise too. He just gave us so much to learn."

It was a lot of little things and a few big things that added up to a different attitude not only team-wise but with Thompson individually. For him, it was something of a career rebirth after two unproductive and frustrating seasons under Infante.

"Remember, this was a time when no one wanted to really play for the Packers," Thompson said.

Thompson, and many other players of that time, had heard the stories. But it was made famous in 1993 when the Packers stunned the NFL by signing the most sought-after free agent in the game, the Philadelphia Eagles' dominant defensive end, Reggie White, to a four-year contract worth $17 million, an unheard of sum in those early days of unrestricted free agency.

In the press conference announcing his signing, White said what Thompson and many other players had heard time and again.

"It used to be coaches would threaten you by saying, 'If you don't play better, I'm going to trade you to Green Bay,'" White said at the time.

But in 1992, when Holmgren and Wolf took over, they set out to immediately change that perspective and Thompson could feel it.

"Holmgren always said he wanted players who wanted to come to Green Bay," he said.

Holmgren also changed the practice regimen to benefit his players.

"We didn't hit, hit, hit in practice," Thompson said. "He said, 'If you're going to tackle, tackle on Sunday.' He did a lot of things like that. He was a little ahead of his time."

In Holmgren's West Coast offense, he tabbed Vince Workman as his starting halfback and Thompson as fullback in training camp. It was a new, exciting time for Thompson until he suffered a torn quadriceps muscle in early August.

That injury sidelined Thompson for nearly two months and in the meantime Workman and rookie Edgar Bennett developed into a solid halfback-fullback tandem. Thompson eventually got his chance to contribute in a November win over the Eagles when he rushed for 72 yards on 18 carries, rushing for one touchdown and catching a pass for another.

He followed that up the next week with 84 yards on 18 carries against the Lions, easily Thompson's best back-to-back performances of his career.

But he suffered an injured ankle and was used only sparingly the rest of the season as the Packers improved to 9–7.

Thompson came back healthy in 1993 and was anxious to work more with the Packers new, young, reckless, exciting quarterback Brett Favre and an offense that featured a legitimate superstar in wide receiver Sterling Sharpe.

Even today, Thompson remembers the impact a youngster like Favre and veteran like Sharpe had on him.

"The thing about Brett I loved was his competitive spirit," Thompson said. "In this game, sometimes that gets beaten out of you. But Brett brought it back in me. I mean, he'd tell dirty jokes in the huddle. He was tough and he was fun. It was a childish fun. I got a little frustrated after my first two years but both Brett and Sterling brought that spirit back in me again."

So Thompson's expectations were high when the season began. But he sputtered again at the start of the season, gaining just 21 yards in the first five games as Green Bay started 2–3.

But in an experiment that would prove to be the highlight of Thompson's pro career, Holmgren moved him to halfback against the Tampa Bay Buccaneers and he exploded for 105 yards, his first 100-yard rushing performance as a pro after more than three years in the league.

What followed was the most consistent series of games in Thompson's career that included his second, and last, 100-yard performance in the home finale. On a frigid afternoon at Lambeau Field, Thompson ran for 101 yards and the Packers blanked the Los Angeles Raiders, helping seal a playoff berth for the Packers.

Thompson was Green Bay's leading rusher that season with 654 yards and three touchdowns. He was also the team's leading rusher in the playoffs, running for a total of 69 yards in a win over the Lions and loss to the Cowboys and catching twelve passes.

But the second half of that season would prove to be the pinnacle for Thompson. The Packers drafted two running backs in 1994, Dorsey Levens and LeShon Johnson, and signed a free agent, Reggie Cobb, making it clear to Thompson that his days with the team might be numbered.

He was right as general manager Ron Wolf decided not to re-sign the veteran. However, late in training camp, he was re-signed only to be waived. Eventually, he'd be signed and released three times, the last in January 1995 as the Packers prepared for the playoffs, earning him the good-natured nickname "Butcher Block" among his friends.

After a promising 1993 season, Thompson would carry the ball only two more times (for minus 2 yards) the rest of his Packers' career, which ended after the 1994 season.

He signed on with the Chicago Bears and Carolina Panthers but didn't stick. Injuries caught up with him including a bad hip that convinced him it was time to move on.

"I was done and I kind of knew it," he said. "But you always think there may be a chance to play a little bit longer. Then I saw the X-ray of my hip and I said, 'That's it.'"

Fortunately for Thompson, a native of Rochester, Minnesota who lives in the Twin Cities today, he long ago knew that football would not last forever. So during his career, he began volunteering with a nonprofit organization in the Twin Cities called Bolder Options, which helps at-risk kids by focusing on healthy youth development.

It features a mentoring program for kids ages seven to seventeen and works to keep kids from dropping out of school and helps them make positive choices.

"I noticed the difference it made in kids' lives," he said. "It grew on me quickly and I went from program manager to executive in about three years. It's built into my life now."

Thompson said more than 2,700 kids went through the program last year and there are nearly 400 kids currently in the program.

As executive director, and still a well-known and respected face in Minnesota, Thompson can be found around the community advocating for the program and, as with all nonprofits, seeking funding for the program.

"People think it's my fundraiser but it's not," Thompson said. "I became a nonprofit from the school of hard knocks."

Thompson has also been the longtime radio color analyst for University of Minnesota football games.

"I have my wife and four kids and everything I do now is extremely important to me," he said.

But he will never forget his days with the Packers and still wonders what might have been.

"I don't hide that at all," he said. "I saw this team go to the Super Bowl [in 1996] and it's like, 'Oh my God.' But it is what it is."

Where Have You Gone?

KEN BOWMAN

"My life's almost been too good."

KEN BOWMAN

Position: Center. Ht: 6'3" Wt: 230

Born: December 15, 1942. Packers career: 1964–73.

Career Highlights: Eighth-round draft pick of the Packers in 1964 from the University of Wisconsin . . . a 10th-round draft pick of the Jets in the AFL . . . Wore No. 57 . . . In recent years has been given more credit, along with guard Jerry Kramer, for throwing key "Ice Bowl" block that allowed Bart Starr to score . . . Inducted into Packers Hall of Fame in 1981.

There was always something a little bit more to Ken Bowman than football. Sure, he was a gifted, and underrated, center who worked his way as a rookie into the starting lineup of one of the great teams in league history—and stayed for ten seasons.

But football never really defined Ken Bowman because he wouldn't let it. Football was always a means to an end for the University of Wisconsin graduate who went on to a stellar career in the law.

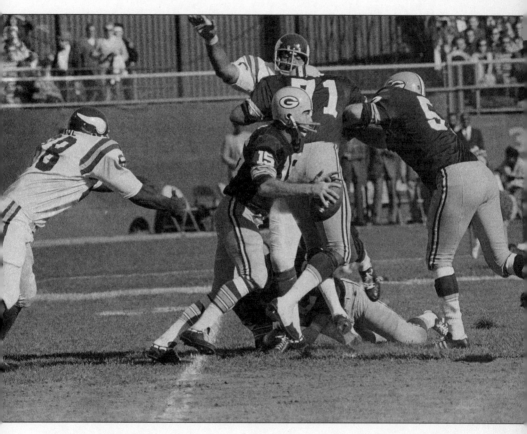

Game action from 1970. Francis Peay (71) and Ken Bowman, right, block the Vikings' Gary Larsen as Bart Starr picks up enough yardage for the first down. (AP Photo/Paul Shane)

"Maybe that's why I have so much empathy with the young people I represent [in court]," said Bowman, who lives in Oro Valley, Arizona, outside Tucson with his wife Rosann. "I was the only member of my family to get a college degree."

And that college degree was everything to Bowman, who even now remembers the promise his dad made to him when he was a kid.

"He said if I was a good enough athlete, they'd find a way to get me into college," Bowman said. "My dad said the key to success was a college education."

So he found a way, first earning his undergraduate degree at the University of Wisconsin and then deciding as a rookie that he was going to get a law degree. And after taking courses at both DePaul University and Northwestern University, during his off-seasons from the Packers, he finished up at Wisconsin, gaining his law degree in 1972.

For Bowman, football provided that mechanism he needed to do what he believed really mattered—and that was becoming a lawyer and, eventually, a judge.

"You've got to try and lighten some people's loads," he said.

Bowman came to football almost by accident. After his father's promise that if he excelled in a sport they'd find a way to get him to college, he began checking out sports as a ninth-grader.

"I tried basketball and track and I tried football and that seemed to be a good fit," Bowman said. "The coach put me in at fullback and my dad said, 'That's great. You're going to get the ball a lot,' and I said, 'I will?' I didn't know a lot about football then."

The next season, as a sophomore at Rock Island High School in Illinois, there were four fullbacks on the team.

"The coach then was a guy named Sonny Franks and he put all four fullbacks on the goal line and made us run to the 40-yard line," Bowman said. "I was last and he said, 'You're my center.' At the time, I looked at it as a demotion."

But even then, Bowman knew he could use his new position to his advantage.

"Being a good center, if you're a decent athlete, you can shine," he said. "It puts a premium on being smart. You can outsmart the other guy."

Bowman was a good enough high school center that he earned his dad's admiration and a scholarship to Wisconsin, where he was a star on the Badgers' 1962 Rose Bowl team that lost to Southern California.

In college, Bowman was already looking to the future.

"I could only enroll in physical education and I didn't want to be a physical education teacher when I graduated," he said. "But if I got A's and B's I'd be able to transfer to the College of Letters and Sciences and that's what I did. But I could only get a sociology degree in four years."

With his degree and an eye to pro football, Bowman was drafted by the New York Jets of the American Football League and in the eighth round by the Green Bay Packers of the more established National Football League.

Bowman decided to sign with a Packers team that was near the pinnacle of its powers. Under coach Vince Lombardi, the Packers had won NFL Championships in 1961 and 1962. In 1963, the Packers were 11–2–1 and missed the playoffs only because they lost twice to the eventual world champion Chicago Bears.

So the rookie joined the juggernaut in 1964, expecting to learn behind veteran center Jim Ringo. But in a story that took on mythical proportions over the years, Ringo supposedly went into Lombardi's office with an agent after the 1963 season seeking a raise. Lombardi was allegedly so angry, he excused himself from the office and a few minutes later returned to tell Ringo he'd been traded to the Philadelphia Eagles. It's a story Bowman still believes.

That's why in the 1964 draft, the Packers selected three centers—Jon Morris, Bill Curry, and Bowman. Morris ended up signing with the AFL's Boston Patriots, leaving Curry and Bowman to battle it out for the center spot.

"If you were a rookie, you didn't start for Lombardi," Bowman said. "But he needed a center."

Veteran Bob Skoronski started that first season and Bowman the next year and Curry the year after that before Bowman settled in for a long, productive career.

Meanwhile, Bowman continued to pursue his future, specifically looking at careers in law or medicine.

"It didn't matter to me," he said. "I just wanted that education."

That's because he knew that his first contract, which paid him what seemed like a decent salary of $12,000, would not last him long after football.

So starting in his NFL offseason, Bowman began his quest for a law degree at Wisconsin. He was even told by then University of Wisconsin law school dean George Young that he might well have to quit football if he wanted to pursue a law degree.

But Bowman figured he could do both so he dove in, spending two semesters at DePaul and another at Northwestern, though no one knew he was actually an NFL player. He even graduated cum laude while still playing.

Through all that, he also had to deal with the force of nature that was Vince Lombardi. And unlike many former players, who talk of Lombardi in reverential tones and as the man who changed their lives, it wasn't necessarily like that for Bowman.

"He was a coach," he said. "I could never understand why so many of the older guys were afraid of him, He's there to basically help you to win a championship and he did everything he could to make that happen. I remember during one training at St. Norbert [College, the Packers longtime training facility], one of the older guys and I were out walking. We were eating ice cream cones and were just walking around. Here comes Lombardi and we say 'Hi coach.' I look around at the older player and I said, 'Where's your ice cream cone?' He saw Lombardi coming and he threw it in the bushes. I didn't understand that. I guess I was way too dumb to be afraid of him."

But not always.

He recalled another story when, during a film session. Lombardi quizzed Bowman on a particular play.

"So I said, 'I'm going to block the middle linebacker . . .'"

But Lombardi kept re-running the sequence and Bowman didn't know why.

"It took me three times to realize he was waiting for me to say 'Yes sir,'" Bowman said. "So many guys loved him like a father. He used to chew my ass up one side and down the other and I thought, 'That's not like any father I had.'"

But he also remembers those times when Lombardi could indeed bring grown men to do things they may not have thought themselves capable.

"When he started practice he'd kill you those first fifteen minutes," he said. "He'd have us do these drills called 'ups and down' and he'd get us so mad at him. Your mind just goes blank. That's when he'd start preaching. He'd say, 'Gentlemen, there will be times this season when you'll need this because the other team will be more tired than you are.' He made believers out of all of us. He'd also run film of the Packers sweep and then show other teams running it. He'd say, 'Gentlemen, every team runs this now but nobody runs it like the Green Bay Packers.' You just wanted to go out and prove it.'"

Perhaps that mental and physical toughness was nowhere more in evidence than December 31, 1967, in the game that forever became known as the "Ice Bowl."

The Packers were clearly reaching the end of their league domination. They were an old, injured group but still had enough left to host the Dallas Cowboys for the NFL Championship Game, which was played in wind chills which, at the time, were measured at minus 44 degrees.

In a play forever etched in NFL history, Packers quarterback Bart Starr snuck into the end zone with thirteen seconds remaining to give Green Bay the 17–14 win. Right guard Jerry Kramer is generally credited with throwing the block on Dallas's Jethro Pugh that allowed Starr to score, but as the years went by, it became clear that Bowman and Kramer performed a textbook double team on Pugh to open the hole.

When Kramer was summoned for a national TV interview after the game, Bowman teased him, telling him to make sure to say it was a double team. Kramer failed to mention it and, for years, it bothered Bowman that he didn't receive the credit he felt he deserved. But that was years ago and Bowman only laughs at the memory.

What no one knew at the time was that touchdown ended an era. The Packers went on the next week to beat the Oakland Raiders in the second Super Bowl. But Lombardi had all but decided at that stage he was done coaching after nine remarkable seasons.

"I think the older guys saw it coming," Bowman said. "I didn't. We had a good run and I couldn't see him quitting at the top like that."

But he did, stepping away as head coach in 1968 to become Packers general manager and handing the coaching duties to his longtime defensive coordinator Phil Bengston.

"I knew it was the end of an era," Bowman said. "Phil was a very good coach but he was no Vince Lombardi. Phil was a nice, mild-mannered guy. He was very business-like."

Bowman continued to anchor the Packers offensive line through a transitional period that saw them sputter through four ineffective seasons.

In 1972, two things happened that impacted Bowman dramatically. The first was he earned his law degree and, not surprisingly, was named a player representative on the players' union executive committee. The second was the Packers, under coach Dan Devine, with a great running game and very little else, posted a 10–4 record and returned to the playoffs.

In some ways, this trip to the playoffs may have meant more to Bowman than any of the others because it was so unexpected and because it relied so much on running the ball, which was what Bowman enjoyed the most.

But the Packers were ousted quickly from the playoffs by the Washington Redskins, who employed a seven-man front to stop Green Bay's potent running attack. Even during the game, Bowman begged Devine to throw the ball more but he refused due to his lack of confidence in quarterback Scott Hunter.

"It would have been pitch and catch," he said. "I still don't understand it."

By then Bowman's interest in players' rights was growing and he was named vice president of the Players Association. In 1974, Bowman was front and center of a players' strike that lasted from July 1 to August 10 to protest restrictions placed on free agents.

"I got a bunch of guys arrested in 1974 [including himself]," said Bowman, who could be seen picketing outside Lambeau Field nearly every day.

Once the strike ended, the damage had already been done. Bowman returned to the facility only to be told he had failed his physical due to a bad back.

"They sent me to St. Mary's Hospital and had me dressed up like a Christmas turkey," he said. "There was nothing wrong with my back and everybody knew it. I was discharged and Dan Devine said don't come over to the Packers building. That's the way I left the Packers organization."

Convinced he could still play and anxious to prove it to the Packers, Bowman signed with the Hawaiians of the World Football League.

"I just wanted to prove there was nothing wrong with my back," he said.

Bowman relished the warm weather after ten years in Green Bay, but the league was doomed almost before it started and it folded after about half a season.

"I can't say there were hard feelings with the Packers," Bowman said. "I knew [the strike] wouldn't go unnoticed. I had given ten years of service to the Packers but there were no hard feelings. I understood their position."

Bowman returned to Green Bay in 1976 and ran unsuccessfully for the state senate and then opened his own law firm. In 1994, Bowman and his wife moved to Arizona where he joined the Public Defender's Office of Pima County.

"All I told them was that I wouldn't take any capital [death sentence] cases," Bowman said. "I told them I come from a civilized state where we don't kill people."

In 2005, he became a special magistrate and works about two days a week.

"I enjoy it," he said. "I'm very happy with my life and I'm glad the good lord gave me the size and speed to play football. My life's almost been too good."

VINCE WORKMAN

"They gave me a chance."

VINCE WORKMAN

Position: Running back. Ht: 5'10" Wt: 215

Born: May 9, 1967. Packers career: 1989–92.

Career Highlights: Played 56 games for the Packers . . . Rushed for 927 yards and 10 touchdowns and caught 97 passes for five touchdowns . . . Fifth-round draft pick of Packers in 1989 out of Ohio State . . . Played for three other NFL teams . . . Wore No. 46.

The call came when Vince Workman least expected it. "It was 1997 and I was back in Ohio," he said.

He found himself in the same position as so many other athletes who wanted to still play the game they loved but due to circumstances, bad luck, or, more often than anything, injury, it just wasn't happening. And that's exactly the situation Workman, a running back who played four seasons with the Green Bay Packers, two seasons with the Tampa Bay Buccaneers and parts of two other seasons with the Carolina Panthers and Indianapolis Colts, found himself.

Vince Workman, left, and Tony Mandarich, right, talk as they leave the Lambeau Field dressing room in 1989. (AP Photo/Bill Waugh)

He was still only twenty-eight years old and entering what should have been the prime years of his career. Instead injuries, including a damaged shoulder and, more seriously, a neck problem, had forced him to consider that a pro football career that always seemed like it was just going to take flight was instead coming to an end.

"I was training like I was going to play again," he said. "I was recovering from a neck injury but I wasn't sure any team would take a chance on me with a neck injury. I knew it was time to hang it up."

So he returned to the place that always gave him the most solace—Columbus, Ohio—where he had starred for the Ohio State Buckeyes in the mid 1980s. Here, maybe, he could find the opportunity to start the second part of his life. But it wasn't quite working out that way.

"I was in engineering sales," Workman said. "But nothing was filling the void. I missed football."

And that's when it happened.

"Out of the blue my agent called and said he'd gotten a call from Reggie McKenzie [the Packers director of player of personnel]. Reggie wanted to know if I was still interested in playing football. I said, 'Are you kidding?'"

It wasn't an opportunity to suit up again and play—those days were over and Workman knew it. But it was the next best thing for a guy who couldn't get football out of his system—player evaluation.

"Reggie wanted me to break down film on four college players and write reports on each player," Workman said. "I had from 6 a.m. to 6 p.m. to do it."

He submitted the reports and in a few days he was offered a job as a scout. It was a position he held for six years with the

Packers, establishing himself as a solid evaluator of college talent and giving him a way to stay in the game he still loved.

"It had never crossed my mind to do that," Workman recalled. "I asked Reggie a few years later about why he thought of me for that job. He said 'I'd interviewed a few guys but both Ron and I remembered you.' Ron remembered I was a hard worker and had good integrity."

Workman laughed.

"I remember my girlfriend always said to be on my good behavior because you never know who's watching," he said. "I guess this was one of those times."

Hard work and integrity were indeed hallmarks of Workman's career, especially with the Packers where he took the ups and downs in stride and made the best of them.

Workman came to the Packers as an unheralded fifth-round draft pick in 1989, part of that draft class that also featured Tony Mandarich, the first-round selection that overshadowed just about everything else in the draft.

Back in the days before twenty-four-hour draft coverage and cell phones, Workman was home in Ohio when Willie Peete, the Packers' running backs coach, called at night and asked if he'd like to play for the Packers. Of course, he said he would.

His rookie season was an eye-opener as he watched the Packers seemingly rally every week for improbable wins. And though he played sparingly (he only carried the ball four times for 8 yards but he was the team's primary kick returner) it was all a good experience and he soaked it in like a sponge.

The Packers posted a 10–6 record and would have made it to the playoffs if the results of another game fell their way.

"I think it was Cincinnati against Minnesota and if the Bengals won we'd be in the playoffs," Workman said. "We all went over to [linebacker] Tim Harris' house to watch that game. The Vikings won."

But Workman figured he'd gotten in on the ground floor of something special with these Packers—a team with a talented coach in Lindy Infante and a great quarterback in Don Majkowski.

"It was interesting," Workman said. "I think because of that success we'd had the year before, some guys came and were a little complacent."

That complacency, in some ways, manifested itself in holdouts by several veterans, including Majkowski, Harris and several offensive linemen. So whatever continuity had been built from the magical 1989 was all but gone by 1990. And it showed.

The Packers struggled almost from the beginning, finishing 6–10, including a five-game losing streak to end the season. Workman again spent much of his time on special teams, rushing for only 51 yards on eight carries and catching four passes.

Ironically, it was 1991, when the Packers hit rock bottom under Infante, that Workman's career finally began to take off.

"I personally had a good year but as a team we really struggled," he said. "We had a lot of injuries that year. Tim Harris was hurt so was [fullback] Brent Fullwood. Majkowski was hurt. It was a carousel of quarterbacks that year (indeed the Packers had three quarterbacks start games that season). Injuries played a huge part in that season."

Workman found his way into the starting backfield, rushing for 237 yards and seven touchdowns and, more telling, catching 46 passes for another 371 yards and four scores. He didn't know it at the time, but it was his ability to catch the ball out of the backfield that would allow him to expand his role with the Packers the following year.

After the 1991 season, Infante was fired and new general manager Ron Wolf hired Mike Holmgren, the offensive coordinator with the San Francisco 49ers and considered perhaps the top young head coaching prospect in the league.

"I really liked Coach Infante," Workman said. "He was great to me and loyal to his players. But I knew there was a possibility he'd be fired. Ron Wolf had been hired and you knew he was going to make changes. You bring in a guy like that and expect everything to stay the same. That wasn't going to happen. Lindy was more of a veteran players' coach and I think a few of the veterans took advantage of that loyalty."

And while Infante had a hand in drafting him and working him into the offense, Workman wasn't necessarily upset to see a change at the top.

"It was definitely a refreshing change," he said. "In terms of style of coaching, Lindy was more old school. He thought nothing of two-and-a-half to three-hour practices but Holmgren came in and said we'd practice for an hour-and-a-half. He said you'd get in condition during practice. It was a new start and it was refreshing. We felt a lot fresher and when it came time for the game, we were ready to go."

Workman was also excited by the possibility of finally utilizing his pass receiving skills in Holmgren's new offense.

"My receiving skills were a big part of the reason why I was drafted in the first place," he said.

And he would finally get a chance to prove it in the season-opener, and Holmgren's debut as an NFL head coach, in September 1992. Indeed, a blueprint of what Holmgren, and the future Packers team, would accomplish could be seen in that game against the Minnesota Vikings.

Workman was, well, the workhorse as he rushed 25 times for 89 yards and caught 12 passes for another 50 yards. And though the Packers lost 23–20 in overtime, the template for future success was there for all to see. The so-called West Coast offense would utilize the short passing game to pick up the same number of yards as the running game. But it also had the ability to pick up major chunks of yardage in the way the run could not. It would be a new way to move the ball and Workman was thrilled with the turn of events.

Indeed, the 12 passes he caught has held up through the 2014 season as a team record for running backs and he figured there would be even more opportunities.

"It was a different attitude, a different mentality," Workman said. "These guys came from the 49ers and they knew how to win. And Ron Wolf changed the culture in Green Bay."

Workman said that change could be seen in even the smallest ways.

"There weren't a lot things for African Americans to do in Green Bay, but he'd have African American barbers come up from Milwaukee just to cut our hair," he said. "That meant a lot."

The Packers also had African American offensive and defensive coordinators [Sherm Lewis and Ray Rhodes] and suddenly a place where many black players didn't think about playing became an option. That was never more in evidence than in 1993 when Eagles defensive end Reggie White, the top free agent on the market, shunned the powerful 49ers and Redskins and signed with the Packers, further changing the culture.

But in 1992, Workman saw the future and he liked it. That future looked even more interesting three weeks into the season when Majkowski, whom Holmgren was reluctantly starting at quarterback mostly because he couldn't trust anyone else yet, badly injured his ankle in a home game against the Cincinnati Bengals.

Faced with few options, Holmgren inserted the young, untested but intriguing Brett Favre, a player Wolf thought so highly of that he gave up a first-round draft pick to the Atlanta Falcons to acquire him that offseason.

"Guys on the team had trouble pronouncing his name," Workman. "But he brought such an attitude. It was just fresh."

Workman was on the field in the final seconds of the game when Favre's legend took root. A touchdown pass in the final seconds led to a 24–23 win, Holmgren's first as a head coach, and Favre didn't leave the field for almost twenty years.

"Still unbelievable," Workman said.

With Favre running the show, the Packers' fortunes began to change. Workman solidified his role as the Packers top running back over veteran Darrell Thompson and rookie Edgar Bennett. Through 10 games, Workman rushed for 631 yards (including his first career 100-yard rushing game in November against the Lions).

But two weeks after that, in a game against the Philadelphia Eagles at Milwaukee County Stadium, Workman ran into the line, heard a crack, felt the pain, and collapsed. He tried to return to the game but couldn't, and at halftime he was told he suffered a separated shoulder and a broken bone in his shoulder plate. His season was done and he was placed on injured reserve. Amazingly, even though he missed the final five full games that season, he still ended up as Green Bay's leading rusher that season.

"I never fully recovered from the shoulder but I wanted to play at the end of the '92 season," said Workman, who watched as the Packers posted a 9–7 record and barely missed the playoffs. "I wanted to be a part of it."

What he didn't know then was that he'd played his last game for the Packers.

That offseason the Packers traded for John Stephenson, a big 210-pound back from the New England Patriots.

"I weighed about 195 pounds and the other backs on the team weighed about 210 pounds," Workman said. "I felt I could be a starting running back in the league but that wasn't my strength. Catching the ball out of the backfield was."

Workman looked at his options as a free agent, visiting the Miami Dolphins and Tampa Bay Bucs, but his hope was to return to the Packers.

"I didn't want to leave," he said. "I knew good things were going to happen and I wanted to be a part of it. But I looked at the writing on the wall."

Because of his close ties with Willie Peete, his first running backs coach in Green Bay who now had the same job in Tampa, Workman decided to sign with the Buccaneers. He had two solid seasons with the Bucs, another team that was trying to rebuild after years of futility.

Meanwhile, he watched from a distance as the Packers continued to improve. After two years in Tampa, Workman went to the Carolina Panthers and then the Indianapolis Colts. But a ruptured disc in his neck finally ended his career in 1996, ironically the same season when the Packers won the Super Bowl and Favre won his second straight league MVP award.

That's when Workman, reluctantly, began to look after life after football and when the Packers, again, came calling.

Workman was hired full time as a scout in 1999 and his respect for Wolf remains as strong as ever.

"Ron Wolf is still the greatest talent scout I've ever been around," he said.

When Wolf retired from the Packers in June 2001, head coach Mike Sherman also assumed the role as general manager and he asked Workman to step away from his role as a scout and take over as the Packer assistant strength and conditioning coach.

"I was a little baffled," Workman said. "But I did it."

He stayed in that position until 2005, when Sherman and his entire staff were fired.

Since then Workman has worked in the field of personal training but remains interested, under the right circumstances, in returning to scouting.

"I still hang with the Packers scouts and I still have a desire to be a scout," he said. "I was around the game and I liked that."

But he couldn't devote the time and attention necessary to be an NFL scout because of his son, Vincent III, who was a rising young football player at a high school in Green Bay.

"My situation was different," he said. "I was a single parent and I didn't want to uproot him. It was a sacrifice not to pursue it but it was the right thing to do."

His son eventually played football at Mankato State in Minnesota and Workman went on to work in a sports medicine facility in Wisconsin and then as an independent contractor in Stamford, Connecticut.

These days, he's back in his native Ohio as the owner of Peak Performance personal training. But he admits he still has the desire to get back into football.

"I'm still in contact with the [Packers] organization because they're a class act," said Workman, who has attended several Packers games in recent seasons. "If the opportunity presents itself, I'll look into it. I could pursue it but I'm in a good place now."

FRANK WINTERS

"It's been a remarkable ride."

FRANK WINTERS

Position: Center. Ht: 6'3" Wt: 290

Born: January 23, 1964. Packers career: 1992–2002.

Career Highlights: *Pro Bowl selection in 1996 . . . Inducted into Packers Hall of Fame in 2008 . . . Selected by Cleveland in 10th round of 1987 draft . . . Started 141 of 156 games with Packers . . . Wore No. 52.*

To this day, Frank Winters isn't really sure where one of the great nicknames in sports history came from. And, also to this day, it's hard to know if it's a nickname the rugged, blue-collar player tried to keep at arm's length.

Some believe it was television analyst John Madden who dropped the nickname on the Green Bay Packers' longtime center. Some people think it was longtime friend and teammate Brett Favre who did the deed. After all, Favre had a nickname for just about everybody he played with—some that could even be repeated in public.

Brett Favre, right, jokes with Frank Winters during a news conference before the Green Bay Packers Hall of Fame induction banquet on July 19, 2008, at Lambeau Field. Favre inducted his longtime teammate and friend. (AP Photo/Mike Roemer)

Most likely the nickname's origin has been lost in time and myth and history.

But, in the end, the details matter little and, even today, to his contemporaries and Packers fans, he is still Joey Bag O' Donuts or the variation, Frankie Bag O' Donuts.

It is not an elegant nickname. It is not graceful, lyrical, or especially complimentary. But perhaps no player in the NFL had a nickname that suited him so perfectly.

Frank Winters played sixteen seasons in the NFL, the last eleven with the Green Bay Packers. He owns one Super Bowl ring, probably should have had a second, and anchored a constantly evolving offensive line over a decade that saw the Packers rise to the heights and crash back down before, again, returning to NFL prominence.

He worked well below the radar in his years in Green Bay, earning just one Pro Bowl berth (in 1996). But he was always there, snapping the ball to Favre, calling out the line assignments and doing whatever was necessary to get the job. For his work, he was named to the Packers Hall of Fame in 2008.

"They always said the NFL stood for 'Not For Long' and that's true," Winters said. "It's something I always tried to prepare for and now that I look at it, I've been very fortunate. It's been a remarkable ride. I appreciated it because I knew football wouldn't last forever."

And while Winters' career lasted longer than many in the NFL, nothing was ever easy for him—not that he expected it ever would be.

A native of Union City, New Jersey, he played his college ball in a place about as far from the streets of New Jersey as could be imagined—at Western Illinois University in the cornfields of Macomb, Illinois.

He was a 10th-round draft pick of the Cleveland Browns and carved out a solid two seasons before going to the New York Giants in 1989 and then on to the Kansas City Chiefs for two more seasons.

At that time, the NFL was still using a version of free agency called "Plan B," which had been established in 1989. It allowed teams to hold onto the rights of thirty-seven players on their rosters. The remaining players were left "unprotected" and could negotiate deals with other teams in the league.

It was the NFL's grudging nod to full-fledged free agency but it did not go far enough in the minds of many players. Indeed, eight players sued the league in the U.S. Federal Court, claiming that Plan B was an unlawful restraint of trade. In 1992, a jury agreed and Plan B was scrapped, opening the door for all players on all teams to negotiate new deals when their contracts expired.

Winters knew all too well about the Plan B process. He had been part of it two years earlier when the Giants had left him unprotected and he ended up going to Kansas City.

Then it happened again two years later when the Chiefs did the same thing. This time, he looked north and decided to sign with the Packers, a team with a new general manager, a new coach and a new young quarterback. It seemed like a team that might be going somewhere and Winters decided he wanted to be part of it.

"We came in with Mike Holmgren and Ron Wolf and they were bringing a new approach," Winters said. "The Packers had had a lot of years of not being successful but it just seemed like something special was happening. I thought this was an organization that had a chance to be great."

But Winters knew it would not happen overnight and he saw plenty of evidence of that.

"There was a pretty big changeover in the roster," he said. "Ron and Mike wanted guys who bought into what they were doing and if you didn't, you weren't there. It was their way or the highway. There was a revolving door and it was an ongoing process."

One guy who may not have necessarily bought what Wolf and Holmgren were selling was a young quarterback named Brett Favre. Possessed with breathtaking ability, Favre came from the Falcons in exchange for a first-round draft pick. And before long Holmgren let Favre know that the success of the Packers, and Holmgren's success as well, would be linked. They would, in short, sink or swim together.

At the same time, Winters and Favre began to develop a friendship. They could not have been more different—with Favre coming from the bayous of southern Mississippi and Winters from the shadow of New York City.

Winters remembered the first time he saw Favre, who had not stayed in shape during a long, bitter, boring season with the Falcons. He had let his weight get away from him and in Green Bay he tipped the scales initially at 250 pounds, causing Winters to wonder if he was a linebacker.

But for whatever reason, the two newcomers connected. They traveled together in the offseason, with Winters even traveling down to Mississippi to the area known as Stinking Springs where they'd go fishing. Winter still remembers alligators coming right up to their boat and Favre just laughing.

The two men would room together during training camp, and on the road they had stuck together through thick and thin. Winters was with Favre in 1996 when the quarterback went to a drug rehab center to kick his addiction to painkillers. Favre consoled Winters when Winters' brother John died just days before Green Bay's appearance in Super Bowl XXXI.

It's a subject that over the years Winters has grown weary of dissecting and discussing.

"He just wants to enjoy life," Winters said of his friend. "Brett does a lot for a lot of people that no one ever really knows about. He has a life after football now and he's a guy who just wants to relax."

But for eleven years, the two were part of some special times with the Packers.

Winters eventually slid in as the Packers starting center in 1993 and earned a reputation of being a tough, hard-nosed, perhaps occasionally dirty player. But it was the only way he knew how to play and it fit the Packers changing mentality perfectly.

Winters remember that while the Packers continued to improve, there remained an impediment—the Dallas Cowboys.

"It was always the Cowboys," Winters recalled. "We knew the Cowboys were the benchmark."

Indeed, in a three-year period from 1993 to 1995, the Packers played the Cowboys three times in the playoffs—all in Dallas—and could not beat them.

"If we could have just gotten them in Green Bay," Winters mused.

A loss to the Cowboys in the 1995 NFC title game was particularly tough because many Packers felt they had outplayed the Cowboys that day but still couldn't get over the hump.

By 1996, the Cowboys star had fallen and the Packers rolled past the 49ers ("We never had much trouble with the 49ers," he said), and the Carolina Panthers to reach the Super Bowl.

And for Winters, who had bounced around the league for years without really enjoying great success, this was the ultimate.

Indeed for Winters, like many of the players on that team, winning the NFC Championship in frozen, raucous Lambeau Field in front of adoring fans may have even topped the Super Bowl. The Packers would go on to beat the New England Patriots for their first world title in twenty-nine years but already many of the players were looking to the next season. That's because they knew, as any player in that circumstance knows, that legacy matters.

Winning one title could be the result of luck or circumstance. But two straight titles? That's the sign of a team for the ages. And that's the message Holmgren and Wolf tried to convey to the team as the 1997 season dawned. Make this one special, show the world.

Wolf knew he had assembled another great team, indeed he saw it as a better team than the one that had won it all the year before.

Winters saw that, too.

"I think it was a better team," he said. "There were no weaknesses."

And they lived up to it, rolling to a 13–3 regular season record, cruising through the playoffs, and meeting the underdog Denver Broncos in the Super Bowl.

But instead of making their mark as one of the great teams in history, the Packers fell to John Elway and the Broncos, 31–24. It's a loss that even today rankles many of those who were involved.

In a postgame interview, Wolf summed it up with his famous quote about the Packers legacy: "We're nothing but a fart in the wind."

Winters still thinks about that loss, too.

"I can't take anything away from how good winning that first one felt," he said. "But that second one . . ."

He pauses.

"You can say you're the better team, but you have to prove it and we didn't do that. And I think about that. To have it slip through your hands like, it's gut-wrenching. It was great to win one and I guess there has to be a winner and loser. But . . ."

It only got worse the next season.

Winters missed the final few games with a broken leg and the Packers were ousted from the playoffs by the 49ers on a last-second touchdown that, in more ways than one, seemed to bring an era to an end.

Barely a week after the loss, Mike Holmgren left the Packers to take over as general manager and coach of the Seattle Seahawks. It's a move that puzzled and hurt many players, including Winters.

"I think that was tough for the team to accept," Winters said. "You don't see coaches leave when they've been that successful. Guys usually remain. There was a bitter taste in our mouths, but it was disappointing. There were still a lot of good years left in players."

Former Packers defensive coordinator Ray Rhodes, who had just been fired as head coach of the Philadelphia Eagles, was hired by Wolf to replace Holmgren, hoping to instill a toughness that he thought the team had lost in recent seasons.

It didn't work out as he'd hoped.

"You could feel it had changed," Winters said. "It just wasn't quite as regimented as it had been."

If anything, the Packers were even less disciplined under Rhodes and by the end of an 8–8 season, Green Bay's worst since 1991, Wolf realized he'd made a mistake and he made another change.

This time he brought in another former Packers assistant coach, Mike Sherman, who was the offensive coordinator for the Seattle Seahawks, to assume the role.

But the years and changes had worn away at Winters. He had played through injuries and adversity but time was catching up to him.

"The games take a toll," he said. "After the 2000 season, I had played the whole season, but I told Mike Sherman I was thinking of retiring. He talked me into coming back for one more year but it wasn't the same. I knew I was done."

He actually returned for two more seasons but at a reduced salary and had to battle with several other younger centers as backup to the new starting center, Mike Flanagan.

Finally prior to the 2003 season Winters was released.

He had been the Packers starting center for most of eleven seasons and had played in the NFL for sixteen, a staggering number especially for an offensive lineman.

"It's just a different game now," he said. "You just don't see guys playing twenty years anymore."

Winters did stay in football for awhile, joining the Indianapolis Colts as an assistant coach, but it wasn't a role he saw himself in for any length of time.

"Now I've been away from the game for so long," he said. "It's a connection business and I don't have a lot of those connections anymore. And you bounce from team to team. It's mind boggling. I just don't know if I have the urge to get back into it."

Winters was inducted into the Packers Hall of Fame in 2008 and, in a touch of irony and controversy, the man he asked to introduce him was his buddy Brett Favre. At that stage, Favre was embroiled in a battle with the Packers regarding the quarterback's decision two months earlier to retire and then his subsequent decision to change his mind as training camp neared.

The Packers had taken Favre at his word that he was going to quit and moved on, handing the quarterback job to longtime understudy Aaron Rodgers.

But Favre wanted to play after all and when he approached the team about reclaiming his job, the Packers balked. The standoff was at its peak when the hall of fame ceremony started. True to his word, though, Favre showed up to introduce his longtime buddy, patting Winters on the stomach during a short talk.

"I knew he'd do it," Winters said. "He told me he would and he's always kept his word with me."

Winters now splits his time between Kansas City and Chicago, keeping an eye on his various business interests that include a number of restaurants and information technology businesses.

"I'd been in the restaurant and business industry for about fifteen years," Winters said. "I've sold several of them and I've also worked with lobbyist firms. I stay busy."

He returns to Green Bay several times a year to reconnect with old friends and teammates from what he still considers the best time of his life.

"I was fortunate to play there," he said. "I've been very fortunate."

MARCO RIVERA

"That's not the way I wanted to go out."

MARCO RIVERA

Position: Offensive guard. Ht: 6'4" Wt: 310

Born: April 26, 1972. Packers career: 1996–2004.

Career Highlights: Sixth-round draft pick of the Packers in 1996 from Penn State . . . Started 111 of 125 games for Packers . . . Pro Bowl selection in 2002, 2003, 2004 . . . All Pro in 2003– 2004 . . . Ed Block Courage Award winner in 2004 . . . Inducted into Packers Hall of Fame in 2011 . . . Wore No. 62.

There is pain that burrows into the soul and takes up residence. It is pain that cannot be explained to anyone but those who have suffered through it. It is pain that becomes part of your life, just like breathing and eating and sleeping.

"You're like a wounded animal," said Marco Rivera, who is now on a first-name basis with the kind of pain that changes your life and, in Rivera's case, ended his career.

But back surgery in late 2014, in which he went through vertebrae fusion, seems to have done the trick.

"I feel really good," he said "It's holding up."

But he has been down this road before and knows how everything could change, again, with the wrong move, a misstep, an ill-timed sneeze. *Something.*

But Rivera is where he wants to be right now, living in Dallas with his family and contemplating a return to the second love of his life—coaching.

His first love? That's easy. Playing football. He learned the game playing under Penn State coach Joe Paterno, and then he was drafted by the Green Bay Packers where he took up residence as both a right and left guard and was part of some successful Packers teams.

"I was only as good as the guy to my right and left," Rivera said of his close relationship with his offensive line mates. "I had [center] Frank Winters to my left and I had [tackle] Earl Dotson to my right and I always wanted to make sure I did my job."

Rivera was a sixth-round draft pick of the Packers in 1996, a draft that produced two other eventual offensive line starters in left tackle John Michels and center Mike Flanagan. More important, he joined a Packers team that was poised for greatness.

The pieces were just about in place for Green Bay to make a run at a world championship, and the concern entering that particular draft was finding a left tackle to replace longtime starter Ken Ruettgers, who had just retired.

The Packers knew only too well that they'd go only as far as rising superstar quarterback Brett Favre would take them. Favre was coming off his first of three straight MVP seasons and it was paramount he stay upright and healthy. That meant finding quality offensive linemen to protect him.

Into this cauldron came Rivera, who was no football neophyte, having started three seasons at Penn State. But even he wasn't prepared for what he saw at the next level.

"When I got to Green Bay, I was in such awe," he said. "You walked into the locker room and you saw guys like Brett Favre, Reggie White, Leroy Butler. It was unbelievable. You see the speed and strength of these guys and you say 'Do I belong here?' You think you're strong but then you realize there are several levels of strong and I knew I had a lot of work to do."

Rivera was inactive that entire 1996 season, when the Packers won their first Super Bowl in twenty-nine years. But the experience of watching from the sidelines was invaluable. Indeed, he gained much of his education by watching the defensive side of the ball—more specifically the game's top pass rusher, defensive end Reggie White.

"Just a great player," Rivera said. "Watching Reggie White play football was unbelievable. He could turn a game at any time."

Rivera gained some badly needed experience that offseason by playing for the Scottish Claymores of the World League of American Football where he was named honorable mention all league. The following seasons, he saw his first time with the Packers, mostly on special teams, as Green Bay went to its second straight Super Bowl.

Finally, in 1998, he battled his way into the starting lineup as left guard, beating out Joe Andruzzi. In 1999, he moved over to right guard and entrenched himself and started for three straight seasons. In 2002, he was voted to his first Pro Bowl, despite playing with damaged knees. It would be the first of numerous physical issues that would plague Rivera the rest of his career.

Still, he continued to play, shaking off more knee and developing back problems to start two more seasons.

And from his perspective, he saw the frantic genius that was quarterback Brett Favre. Rivera demurred when asked about some of the best stories about the quarterback, insisting the best ones could never be repeated.

But he remembers all too well what Favre meant to the Packers.

"People lose sight of the fact that he was such a good teammate, such a great competitor," Rivera said. "The Green Bay Packers returned to glory because of Brett Favre. They were in a dark tunnel of nowhere before him. He put them back on the map and changed the whole face of the franchise. A lot of people lose sight of that."

Rivera recalled one story about Favre during a tough divisional game with the Minnesota Vikings.

"I remember this game and the Vikings were moving their safeties up and Brett was calling an audible," Rivera said. "He was calling out this jargon 'red over' and all these other things, it was crazy. Then he pauses and says, 'Go back to the original play . . . set . . . hut.' It was incredible. That play still gained eight yards. Mike Holmgren's face after that was priceless. You thought he'd seen a ghost. But that's who Brett was."

In 2005, after nine seasons in Green Bay, Rivera signed a five-year, $20 million free agent contract with the Dallas Cowboys that included a $9 million signing bonus. It was a deal Rivera couldn't refuse despite his desire to stay in Green Bay.

But the move never panned out as expected.

While running on a treadmill prior to receiving an NFL award in the preseason, Rivera suffered a herniated disk that required surgery. Still he played all season before a neck injury forced him out the final two games of that season.

He played well in 2006 but another back injury in a playoff loss to the Seattle Seahawks was another setback.

"It completely destroyed my back," said Rivera, who wouldn't sit down during that game for fear his back would tighten up and he wouldn't be able to stand up again.

After that game, he had to be physically helped onto the plane for the trip home. He knew then that his career, quite likely, might be over.

"That's not the way I wanted to go out but it just got to the point where my body just gave out," he said.

Another back surgery followed and in June, the Cowboys released Rivera and his career was done.

That began what Rivera called a "two-year spiral" that included surgery, pain medications, and an emotional roller-coaster that had him wondering if he'd ever feel anything close to normal again.

"It took me a few years to get over it," he said. "I was taking pain medication too much."

But in 2009, in the depths of his concern, he was thrown a lifeline by his old college offensive line coach, Tony Sparano, who was coaching the Miami Dolphins.

"He called me and asked if I could come down and help with off-season workouts and the OTAs [organized team activities]," he said. "So I went down and helped. I enjoyed myself but I was in such a lot of pain. I enjoyed it, but my body was not with me."

After helping Sparano in 2009, Rivera's back issues flared again and he stepped away in 2010 in hopes of feeling better.

But in 2011 another former coach came calling and, again, Rivera couldn't say no. Joe Philbin, who had been an assistant coach with the Packers in Rivera's later years, was the Dolphins' new head coach, and he wanted Rivera to help school the offensive line.

It was an opportunity Rivera was anxious to embrace but he just didn't know if he could handle it physically. He got his answer soon enough when, while on vacation with his family, he suffered another back injury.

But the lure was too strong and he'd made a promise to Philbin to help out, so he shot himself up with a series of epidurals and went to Miami.

"I didn't want to tell anybody," he said. "My back was on fire and my legs were weak. I don't think he knew how much pain I was in. I've always had a high tolerance for pain."

Rivera fought that pain and did such a good job as an "assistant to the assistant" that Philbin asked him to commit full time to being a coach.

But by that point, Rivera knew, on several levels, that might not be the best course for him.

That's when he had his third surgery in five years, and he is now waiting to see how his back holds up.

He admits there's much about coaching he enjoys. He remembers when he played for the Packers how he tutored a young and impressive University of Wisconsin guard named Mark Tauscher who was dealing with the same physical and mental issues related to the NFL that Rivera had to deal with as a rookie.

"I was always working with him and making sure he was OK," Rivera said. "I guess that was the coach in me. I guess I was kind of the coach on the field."

And Rivera is also drawn to the technical aspects of the game that so many former players want nothing to do with.

"I love breaking down film," he said. "It's part of my life. One of my strengths has always been that I need to know everything I can about an offense."

So the issue of whether he wants to, or even can, commit to coaching full time was still up in the air.

"Do I want to bounce around as a lot of assistant coaches do?" he said. "I've been struggling with that. It's a big decision because I have three boys at home and a wife."

But the decision may end up being out of his hands if his back, once again, erupts in pain.

"Nobody can understand unless they've been through it," he said.

BRYCE PAUP

"I want to help keep people from making the stupid mistakes I made."

BRYCE PAUP

Position: Linebacker. Ht: 6'5" Wt: 250.

Born: February 29, 1968. Packers career: 1990–94

Career Highlights: Started 41 of 64 games for Packers . . . Recorded 193 tackles and 32-and-a-half sacks . . . Sixth-round draft pick in 1990 from Northern Iowa . . . Pro Bowl selection in 1994 . . . Wore No. 95.

As he watched from home as the Green Bay Packers won Super Bowl XXXI after the 1996 season, Bryce Paup felt a twinge of longing, jealousy, and, yes, a little anger. He should be there, he thought. He should be celebrating with the guys he had called friends and teammates for five seasons.

But as the Packers players raised the Vince Lombardi Trophy on the confetti-strewn field at the New Orleans Superdome on that January evening in 1997, Paup also knew that everything that had happened to him in his career had happened for a reason.

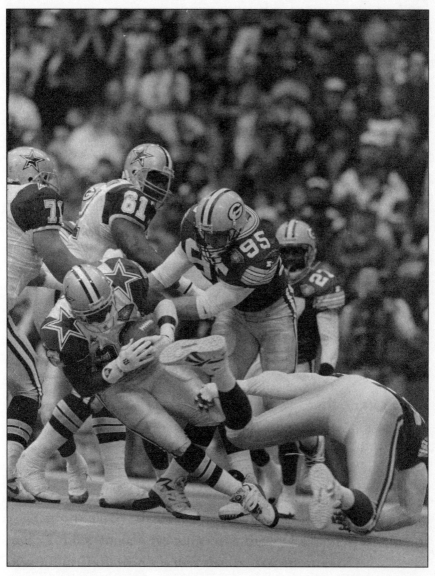

Bryce Paup (95) tackles Emmitt Smith for a loss during 1994 game
action. (AP Photo/Ron Heflin)

"Green Bay is my kind of town," he said. "I mean, I grew up in Iowa. Sure it would have been nice to have been a part of that but part of me was happy for the people who had been there for so long and had a chance to enjoy it."

That's the way Bryce Paup looks at life: Everything works out for the best even if it often doesn't seem like that's the case when it's happening.

Paup enjoyed a superb eleven-year career that included recognition as the Associated Press Defensive Player of the Year in 1995 and four trips to the Pro Bowl. The first five were played in Green Bay, where he evolved from a 1990 sixth-round draft pick without a position to one of the game's most feared pass rushers.

He learned the pro game from a crusty veteran coach named Hank Bullough, refined it when a new regime took over and then left before he could ever really prove just what he could do.

Paup has no regrets save one—the Super Bowl ring every player craves but so few ever receive.

These days, he's found a career he never once considered until he realized that it was exactly what he was suited to do.

"The last thing on my mind was going into coaching," he said. "I kind of backed into it."

Indeed, Paup had retired after the 2000 season and his family still lived in the Green Bay area.

"My boys were getting to an age where they were playing sports and I ran into Greg Rabus [the football coach at East DePere High School] who asked if I'd be interested in coaching. I said I was. It was kind of a feeling-out period for both of us. They wanted to see if they liked what I was doing and I wasn't sure it was what I wanted."

Of course, the young players went through the roof when they saw they might be coached by a former Packers player. But it ended up being more than that.

"I started having a positive impact on kids," Paup said. "It was fun. It kind of snowballed."

Paup got his feet wet as an assistant coach and then moved to become head coach at Green Bay Southwest High School. But even then he wasn't sure it was a commitment he wanted to make.

"At first I didn't want to coach and then I didn't want to be a head coach," he said. "I figured just because you can play doesn't mean you can coach. If you're true to yourself, you'll be true to others. If you want people to lead then you have to show them how to do it."

Paup ended up coaching Southwest for six seasons, taking a program that had struggled for years and transforming it into one of the top prep programs in the state. In his six seasons, Southwest went 43–21 and had back to back 10-win seasons in 2011 and 2012.

But that 2012 season had an impact on Paup.

"We lost in the third round of the playoffs," he said. "I think it was by like three or four points and it really took the wind out of my sails. And I found the enthusiasm wasn't coming back. I didn't want to commit to another season if I wasn't going to give everything I had. For me to keep that passion for coaching, I needed a change."

That spring, Paup also learned that his alma mater, Northern Iowa University (where his close friend Mark Farley was the head coach) was seeking several defensive coaches.

"I had played with Mark and he has coached me a couple of years," Paup said. "It sounded like a great opportunity and I was able to convince my wife."

So now Paup has moved to the next level of a coaching career he wasn't even sure he wanted. As of 2015, he is linebackers coach at Northern Iowa and now people are already asking him if he'd like to be an NFL assistant coach someday.

It's a question that, at least these days, just makes him laugh. "I'm not there yet," he said.

Now that he's had a chance to reflect on the career that he swears he had given no thought, Paup may well realize that being a coach is perhaps the perfect job for him. Calm and reflective and thoughtful, he views coaching as a teaching assignment. Where many coaches may use intimidation or threats as a way to motivate, Paup prefers the hands-on approach, explaining what needs to be done rather than demanding it.

He saw both styles in his playing career in which he spent five years in Green Bay, another three with the Buffalo Bills, two with the Jacksonville Jaguars and a final season with the Minnesota Vikings.

A native of Jefferson, Iowa, a town of 4,000 people located nearly dead square in the middle of the state, Paup became a star at Northern Iowa and caught the attention of a Packers team coming off a stunning and surprising 10–6 season in 1989 under first-year coach Lindy Infante.

The Packers concentrated on defense in the 1990 draft, grabbing six defensive players in its first nine picks. Paup's selection in the sixth round produced little if any reaction and, in truth, Paup wasn't that overwhelmed either.

"I didn't hear a whole lot from the Packers before the draft," he said. "Growing up, I was a Dallas Cowboys fan. I knew where Minnesota was and I knew where Kansas City was. But Green Bay? Not so much. I remember in junior high, my football team was upset with a drill we were doing and he said, 'If Vince Lombardi saw that, he'd roll over in his grave.' I thought, 'So what? Who's that?'"

He learned quickly enough about the Vince Lombardi mystique and what football meant to Green Bay. He also knew that he had a lot to do if he hoped to contribute in professional football.

It did help that a former coach of his, Hank Bullough, was in charge of the Packers defense, and Bullough ran the kind of defense that Paup was familiar with from his days at Northern Iowa.

He played five games that first season but then found his way into the starting lineup for the season opener in 1991 against the Philadelphia Eagles. It ended up being a memorable game for the young linebacker.

In the first quarter, Paup converged on the Eagles' dynamic quarterback Randall Cunningham, who was coming off an NFL MVP season in 1990, and brought him down for his first NFL sack. But as he was bringing Cunningham down, Paup also connected with Cunningham's left knee, tearing his anterior cruciate ligament and ending his season almost before it had begun.

It was an auspicious start for Paup, who would make a name for himself as one of the most disruptive linebackers in the game.

He finished with seven-and-a-half sacks his first season, second on the team behind another rookie linebacker, Tony Bennett.

In 1992, changes overtook the Packers organization with the hiring of Ron Wolf as general manager and Mike Holmgren as head coach. Bullough was out as defensive coordinator and Ray Rhodes, Holmgren's hand-picked choice from the San Francisco 49ers, took over.

Paup recorded six-and-a-half more sacks from his inside linebacker position that season and he was encouraged by the direction the Packers were headed.

But he soon began to get disturbing signs that, perhaps, he was not the kind of player Holmgren and his staff wanted to build a defense around.

"They wanted it to be their team," he said, convinced that players who were drafted before the new staff came in weren't for them. He hoped he was wrong, but as time went by he began to think he wasn't.

"I don't know, if it's me, I think I'd want to win with other guy's people just to show you can do it," he said. "I don't know, if I'm in the same situation back then, maybe I'd think the same way he did."

Paup remembered one incident in practice that involved the player Holmgren had tied his future to, quarterback Brett Favre.

"I remember I'm on the practice field and I beat the offensive lineman and as I'm going by Brett I kind of playfully touched the ball and knocked it out of his hands," he said. "Holmgren stopped practice and he went off on me. He said, 'If you ever do anything like that again, I'll cut you.' And that's when I thought, 'Oh boy.'"

In the 1993 draft, perhaps as a signal to Paup, the Packers drafted linebacker Wayne Simmons in the first round.

That season, Paup was moved to outside linebacker, a position he wasn't familiar, or especially comfortable, with. But he made the move and had the best season of his career, posting a career-high 11 sacks, second only to Reggie White, whom the Packers had signed that offseason to the richest free agent contract in NFL history at the time.

"Then they moved me to middle linebacker," Paup said.

And in 1994, he had the best all around season of his career, posting seven-and-a-half sacks, intercepting three passes, forcing two fumbles, recovering two more fumbles and finishing with 47 tackles. His performance earned him his first trip to the Pro Bowl but Paup and Holmgren, by that point, were not seeing eye-to-eye.

Moving from position to position with nowhere in particular to call home, Paup was growing frustrated not only with his role but with his relationship with Holmgren.

"I'd had shoulder surgery and I went into training camp not very happy," he said of that pivotal 1994 season. "But I admit some of it was self-inflicted."

He said he remembers that when Holmgren put Paup's name on the Pro Bowl voting list it was at defensive tackle, a position he hadn't played at all in Green Bay.

"Who does that?" Paup said. "No one was going to vote for me as a defensive tackle."

He said Holmgren also tried to give his defensive statistics, such as tackles and sacks, to other players so that the Packers could be in a better negotiating position when Paup's deal was up at the end of the year.

Still, Paup had a superb season and seemed poised to earn a substantial raise on a new contract. After all, he provided a decimating pass rush duo with defensive end Reggie White. With White coming from one side (he'd had eight sacks that season as the Packers reached the second round of the playoffs) and Paup coming from the other, they formed what figured to be a nightmarish sack combo to last for years.

Paup thought the same thing. And despite his differences with Holmgren, Paup liked Green Bay, loved the fans and saw that this team was building toward something special.

But Holmgren and Wolf didn't see it that way.

"I brought contract numbers to Ron Wolf and Holmgren," he said. "My intent was to stay in Green Bay so I went out and brought them numbers that I thought were fair to everyone. They didn't even make an offer. There was no opportunity to stay."

And while there was some interest from the Jacksonville Jaguars and Houston Oilers, it was the Buffalo Bills who stepped in with a staggering offer of three years for $7.6 million with a $3.3 million signing bonus.

And while Paup was willing to sign for less to stay in Green Bay, that offer was almost $1 million more a season than the Packers offered. It was no decision.

Paup left Green Bay after five seasons and flourished in Buffalo.

"I wanted to win a Super Bowl in Green Bay," he said. "But you can only make that kind of money for so long. It was disappointing leaving Green Bay but I couldn't turn that down."

In Buffalo, Paup became the player he always felt he could be. In three seasons in Buffalo, he posted 33 sacks, including 17-and-a-half in 1995. He was an All Pro player all three seasons and made the list as one of the top 50 Bills players of all time.

"It worked well for me," Paup said. "Buffalo treated me well."

But while he was putting up the big numbers, he also watched as the Packers took that next step to NFL greatness. In 1995, the Packers went to the NFC Championship Game and the next two years they went to the Super Bowl, winning the first and losing the second.

Paup laughs.

"I've said before that the Packers had to get rid of me to win a Super Bowl," he said.

After three seasons in Buffalo, Paup moved on to play two seasons in Jacksonville and closed out his career in 2000 playing for the Minnesota Vikings. He finished with 75 career sacks, still placing him among the top 75 all time in the NFL.

These days, Paup is happy with his progression in the coaching ranks. He's learned from some of the best in the business—both the good and the bad—when it comes to coaching.

"As a high school coach I learned a lot after getting knots on my head from being stupid," he said. "I've learned it was about character-building and leadership training. I'm here to help people. I want to help keep people from making the stupid mistakes I made."

MARK MURPHY

"I never wanted to feel I'd made it."

MARK MURPHY

Position: Safety. Ht: 6'2" Wt: 200

Born: April 22, 1958. Packers career: 1980–1991

Career Highlights: Undrafted free agent from West Liberty State in 1980 . . . Started 122 of 147 games . . . Posted 20 interceptions and 11 quarterback sacks . . . Inducted into Packers Hall of Fame in 1998 . . . Wore No. 37.

Could a guy like Mark Murphy play in the NFL these days? Even Mark Murphy isn't sure of that. But in 1980, there was indeed a place for a gritty, competitive defensive back from a tiny college in West Virginia. And for twelve years Murphy manned the safety position for an interesting, infuriating and usually entertaining array of Packers teams.

"I played four seasons for Bart Starr, four seasons for Forrest Gregg, four seasons for Lindy Infante, and two weeks for Mike Holmgren," Murphy said with a laugh. "I played for four different head coaches and I say I got them all fired."

Mark Murphy corrals Chicago Bears running back Walter Payton to
bring him up short on a fourth down play on October 22, 1985. (AP
Photo/Charlie Bennett)

But his self-deprecating humor and unassuming ways were what made Murphy a fan favorite for years, because they knew, as he did, that he'd squeezed just about everything from a professional football career that he could have ever hoped.

Even the disease he acquired as a kid, alopecia (a loss of hair), led to his trademark bald head that made him recognizable, and still does, to Packers fans everywhere.

His is a classic underdog tale that, unlike so many, ended in a way that worked for all involved. After his NFL career, he moved into coaching at Malone College in Akron, Ohio and then the University of Akron before settling in as assistant dean of students at St. Vincent-St. Mary High School in Akron, Ohio, where he still coaches the high school football team's defensive backs.

"I don't want to be the head coach," he said. "My job is on the field teaching. I love coaching higher level kids. We've got some pretty talented kids and I love watching them develop. But I really enjoy the kids who really improve from the time they're freshmen to when they become seniors. That's really special."

In fact, Murphy could well be talking about himself and his development from small-college player to a legitimate NFL safety.

Murphy wasn't sure if he'd get an opportunity to show the pros what he could do since he played for an NAIA Division I school, West Liberty State College in Wheeling, West Virginia.

He went undrafted in 1980 and three teams—the Pittsburgh Steelers, Cincinnati Bengals and Green Bay Packers—had been in contact with him as a potential free agent.

"I was thinking about what place would give me the best opportunity," Murphy said. "I looked at Pittsburgh, the defending Super Bowl champs, and I figured it was slim chance. The Bengals had one of the best secondaries in the NFL and I figured that as pretty slim too. But the Packers had drafted four defensive backs so I figured they were probably making some changes. Plus Ross Fichtner, the Packers defensive backs coach, had called me before, during and after the draft so I thought they were interested."

So Murphy signed with the Packers and learned what every other rookie learns immediately.

"The first thing you notice is the size, strength, and speed of the players," he said.

He also learned that he had to develop his skills playing man to man defense, which he didn't do much in college. But Murphy brought an attitude with him that there was nothing he couldn't learn, nothing he couldn't overcome.

Murphy opened the coaching staff's eyes in that training camp, stuck around and, amazingly, found himself on the field for the opening of the Hall of Fame Game, which opens the NFL's preseason.

"That was special to me because it's played in Canton [Ohio] and that's my hometown," he said.

But on the opening kickoff, reality found Mark Murphy.

"We were playing San Diego and this guy hits me so hard and drove me into the sideline and breaks my wrist," he said.

The injury ended Murphy's rookie season but he viewed it as a benefit.

"I got a chance to learn and grow," he said. "I was able to practice so I worked on my man to man coverage skills and got better."

The next season Murphy was healthy and had learned to play both the strong safety and free safety positions, giving him the versatility the Packers couldn't ignore.

"I felt like I caught up pretty quickly," he said. "And then we got receivers like James Lofton and John Jefferson and Phil Epps and I got to practice with some pretty good players."

In 1981, Murphy stepped in at strong safety for the injured Johnny Gray and through the 1991 season, Murphy could always be found in his familiar spot. He did miss the entire 1986 season and part of the '87 season with a broken ankle, but the rest of the time, he was a dependable defender for Packers teams that, in that era, had lots of offense but sometimes struggled on defense.

Perhaps the epitome of that was the 1983 season when the Packers' offense, triggered by quarterback Lynn Dickey and a fleet of great receivers, rung up 429 points (fifth-best in the NFL) and 6,172 yards (second-best in the league behind the San Diego Chargers).

Those Packers could score from just about anywhere on the field and often did. But it proved to be a requirement as the season went on since the defense struggled to stop anyone—allowing 439 points and 6,403 yards, third-worst in the league.

But it was a fun, raucous season that saw the Packers play five overtime games, still the most in NFL history, and win three of them. They were also part of what remains a legendary game in *Monday Night Football* history.

In a game against the defending Super Bowl champion, the equally potent Washington Redskins, the Packers eventually pulled out a 48–47 win, secured only after the Redskins missed a short field goal in the game's final seconds. It's still the highest scoring *Monday Night Football* game in history.

"Oh my God, I do remember that game," Murphy said. "It really did seem like it was a case of the last team that had the ball was going to win."

And while Murphy's seen some of the teams he played for had defensive deficiencies, he points out that in 1984, the Packers led the league in forcing turnovers.

The 1983 team, which finished 8–8, proved to be Bart Starr's final season as head coach and the legendary former Packers' quarterback was fired and replaced with another Packers legend from a bygone era, Forrest Gregg.

Those Packers teams took on more than the personality of the Hall of Fame offensive lineman. Tough, mean and, yes, at times dirty and undisciplined, these Packers were more known for the thermo-nuclear wars they waged with their ancient rivals, the Chicago Bears. Those games featured late hits and brawls that often spilled over after the games.

But the Packers rarely won those games and Gregg had little more success than Starr, posting a 25–37–1 record in four seasons. He was replaced by Lindy Infante but, through it all, Murphy hung on.

"I kept seeing guys who played at major colleges and they're getting released and I played at this little school and I'm still here," Murphy said. "I always said, and I tell my players now, there are only two things you can control—effort and attitude. If you have those you give yourself a chance and I think that's what I was able to do."

But Murphy also understood how fragile and fleeting an NFL career can be.

"It may sound like a cliché but this is how I looked at it," he said. "I really did take it one year at a time. Obviously, they bring in guys every year to try and replace you but I always embraced that. I never wanted to buy a house in Green Bay because I never wanted to feel comfortable. I never wanted to feel I'd made it, because if you think that, then you get complacent."

Murphy was now one of the veterans by the time Infante took over in 1988, but nothing was really changing on the field.

There was one memorable season in four, when the Packers went 10–6 in 1989 yet still missed the playoffs.

And if there was a sore point in an otherwise successful career, it was the fact the Packers didn't get to the playoffs more. Murphy played in one playoff game, against the St. Louis Cardinals, in the strike-shortened 1982 season. He had an interception in that game that the Packers lost.

He'd never see the postseason again and he never quite understood that.

"We had a lot of 8–8 teams," he said. "We had talent on a lot of those teams but we just couldn't get over the hump. We were close but we just couldn't get over the hump. We had good players but just not enough."

Four years later, again, and Infante was out, replaced by a whole new regime and a whole new attitude led by new general manager Ron Wolf and head coach Mike Holmgren.

It was 1992 and Murphy knew the end was coming but, in his view, wasn't there just yet.

He had led the Packers in tackles the year before and was still a reliable safety, and he felt he could provide a veteran presence for a young, developing team.

"I knew I had another year left, tops, in my mind," Murphy said. "I'd had a good season in '91. I knew I was close but it was just a question of whether they were willing to keep a twelve-year guy."

But Murphy got his answer fairly early in camp when Leroy Butler, a second-round draft pick in 1990 who had been a free safety, was moved to Murphy's longtime position.

It wasn't much longer before he was released.

"I didn't leave bitter," Murphy said. "I would have loved to go out on my own terms but they did things the right way and they still do. They felt they needed to make a change and that was OK. It worked out the way it was supposed to work out."

But Murphy wanted to give it one more shot and he tried out with the Pittsburgh Steelers.

The Steelers were looking for someone to help out mostly on special teams and when they asked if he was interested, he said he was and he'd be back the next day.

"I was driving home from Pittsburgh and I stopped in Steubenville, called my agent and said 'I'm done.'"

That's when Murphy faced the issue all former athletes must eventually face—what comes next?

"I said, 'OK, now you've got to find your way.'"

It was soon after when he was contacted about coaching defensive backs at Malone College while also selling real estate in his free time.

"I was going to go into business after football," Murphy said. "But real estate was everything I didn't want. It was nights and weekends."

After a year at Malone, he moved on to coach at Akron but the time commitment was too much for him and, after two seasons, he learned of the opportunity at St. Vincent-St. Mary.

"I came for a year and have stayed ever since," he said with a laugh.

His kids have all graduated from the school and Murphy has even coached his own sons, one of whom, Mark Jr., went on to play defensive back at Indiana University.

"My son, he's different mentally than me," Murphy said. "He's just a sharp kid. He grew up around the game."

Indeed, Murphy speaks with pride of the fact his son would go to bed every night watching film of his dad playing for the Packers.

"He couldn't identify any of the Packers now but he knew all the guys on those teams," he said, laughing. "It was fun coaching him but he's his own person."

He showed that prior to his senior season at IU when he told his dad he probably would not pursue a career in the NFL.

"I think he was feeling me out about it," Murphy said. "But he's had three shoulder surgeries and I think he was done. All I told him was don't look back and have regrets."

Wise words from a dad who has never looked back with regret.

DORSEY LEVENS

"It turned out to be a blessing in disguise."

DORSEY LEVENS

Position: Running back. Ht: 6'1" Wt: 230

Born: May 21, 1970. Packers career: 1994–2001.

Career Highlights: Pro Bowl and All Pro selection in 1997 . . . Drafted by Packers in fifth round of 1994 draft from Georgia Tech . . . Rushed for 3,937 yards and 28 touchdowns . . . Caught 271 passes for 16 touchdowns. Both figures are among Packers all-time best. . . . Inducted into Packers Hall of Fame in 2009 . . . Wore No. 25.

Dorsey Levens is a true believer. He has seen the evidence and he has experienced it too—firsthand and all-too painfully—and he will talk to anyone, anywhere about the dangers involved with football.

"I was talking to the head trainer at the University of North Carolina and he said every time you get your 'bell rung,' that's a concussion," Levens said. "That got me thinking."

Levens spent eleven seasons in the NFL, the first eight with the Green Bay Packers, and he has lost count of the number of times he's had his "bell rung."

Dorsey Levens breaks through the line for a touchdown run against the Detroit Lions, November 21, 1999. (AP Photo/Bill Waugh)

But it's been since he left the game after the 2004 season that he began to understand the full impact of what all those years of collisions truly meant.

He's worried, and he's scared, that he may be part of a growing number of NFL players who will be dealing with the effects of head injuries over a long period.

"I have some symptoms," Levens said. "Not daily and not really bad. But I know I have some. But right now I'm OK."

What concerns him is how long he'll stay that way.

So he's doing what he can to make sure players are informed and receptive to what's going on. Indeed, it works right into what Levens loves best—film and acting and writing.

He has spent his time since football working on a documentary about concussions as well as pursuing a career in acting, directing and writing.

"The goal is to get something bigger," he said. "I've always been a big movie buff and took acting classes for about ten years in Atlanta. I like the fact that you can be somebody else."

But for most of his life, the Syracuse, New York native was a football player—a running back at Notre Dame and then Georgia Tech in college and a fifth-round draft pick of the Packers in 1994 who never quite lived up to his potential, mostly because of the injuries that so concern him now.

He showed flashes of real greatness, both running the ball and catching passes out of the backfield, and in 1996 and 1997, the years the Packers went to the Super Bowl, he was an integral part.

But in 1994, his selection was met with little fanfare. Indeed, the Packers already seemed set at running back. Levens was an intriguing project, an often injured player in college who had to prove he could stay healthy to contribute at this level.

But all Levens knew when he was drafted was how little he knew.

"Oh jeez," he said. "When they told me I'd be drafted by Green Bay I thought 'It's cold.' That's first and foremost. I'd never been to Wisconsin; I just knew it was cold. I had told my agent before the draft that I'd like to go anywhere but Green Bay. It turned out to be a blessing in disguise."

Levens didn't provide much his rookie season, carrying the ball just five times as he tried to figure out exactly what was happening.

"It was a whirlwind," he said. "I didn't know what was good and I didn't know what was bad. I told my friends this was another level. All these guys are good, even the ones who get cut."

But Levens was optimistic about his future because he'd been selected by one of the NFL's great evaluators of talent—general manager Ron Wolf.

"He was really good at what he did and I knew he saw something in me," Levens said.

What he didn't know at the time was that he was part of the process, one of the building blocks of Wolf and head coach Mike Holmgren as they set sights on the long-sought Super Bowl title.

It began their first year together when they took wide receiver Robert Brooks, running back Edgar Bennett and tight end Mark Chmura. It continued in 1993 when they drafted linebacker Wayne Simmons, tackle Earl Dotson and cornerback Doug Evans, and in 1994 Levens joined tackle Aaron Taylor and defensive end Gabe Wilkins. In 1995, cornerback Craig Newsome, fullback William Henderson, linebacker Brian Williams, and wide receiver Antonio Freeman helped complete the puzzle.

But two years before that first Super Bowl, Levens was stuck behind Bennett and unsure what his future held.

Yet it was his versatility, especially his ability to catch the ball out of the backfield, that intrigued Holmgren since his self-styled "West Coast" offense required a back who could catch. His size, 6-foot-1, 240 pounds, also appealed to the Packers and led to his nickname of "Dorse the Horse."

By 1995, Levens' role was coming into focus. In a season that saw the Packers win their first NFC Central title since 1972, he was still the No. 2 back behind Bennett and gained just 120 yards on the ground. But he was becoming skilled out of the backfield as a pass catcher, grabbing 48 passes for 434 yards and four touchdowns. He caught seven more passes in the postseason.

His role continued to grow in 1996 and he formed an impressive tandem with Bennett, who rushed for more than 800 yards, while Levens rushed for more than 500.

And in the NFC title game at frigid Lambeau Field, Levens put on a virtuoso performance, catching five passes for 117 yards, including a remarkable leaping grab over a defender in the end zone for Green Bay's first touchdown of the game. He also rushed for a career-high 88 yards on 10 carries as Green Bay routed the Carolina Panthers and sent the Packers to their first Super Bowl in thirty years.

In Super Bowl XXXI, Levens was the Packers' leading rusher with 61 yards on 14 carries and tied for the team lead in receptions with three. It was a hint of what was to come.

The plan was to use the Bennett-Levens tandem again in 1997 as the Packers sought to lock down back to back world titles. But the plan was scrapped almost before it began when Bennett ruptured an Achilles tendon in the preseason opener, ending his season and, in fact, his career as a Packer.

"It was my breakout opportunity," Levens recalled. "It was my first chance to be a starter. This is what I'd been working toward. I wasn't sure if I'd ever get that opportunity because Edgar could run and catch and was so assignment pure. It was a bad break for him but it did give me a chance."

And he made the most of the opportunity.

Battling an assortment of injuries all season, including a unusual separated clavicle injury, Levens still rushed for 1,435 yards on a staggering 329 carries.

Levens remembers that injury to his shoulder in which even the process of breathing was an issue.

"I remember I got hurt and we had a bye week the next week so I was ready to play the next game, a Monday night game at New England," he said. "Holmgren gave me the ball about 30 times."

Levens fought through the injuries and ran for more than 100 yards six times that season. He also caught 53 passes and was named All Pro and earned a spot in the Pro Bowl for the first and only time in his career as the Packers stormed to a 13–3 record.

He was just as good in the postseason, running for 112 yards against the Tampa Bay Buccaneers and 114 against the San Francisco 49ers and the Packers earned their second straight trip to the Super Bowl.

Levens again played well, rushing for 90 yards and catching seven passes. But he disappeared from the offense as the game went along and, eventually, the underdog Denver Broncos rallied and won, 31–24.

The loss still ticks with Levens all these years later.

"Unfortunately, that's the Super Bowl I remember most," he said. "I think you always remember the losses more. I'm kind of over it but I still won't watch the last ten minutes of it."

The timing could not have been better, or worse, for Levens as he was coming off a career season just as his contract was expiring.

What followed was a protracted and sometimes bitter negotiation between the team and Levens' agent, Hadley Englehard. Levens was seeking a five-year contract worth $25 million and the Packers were only willing to offer $4 million a season.

"The closer I got to thirty, the less chance I had of making big money. I was cognizant of that."

Levens skipped all of the team's offseason workouts as well as most of training camp in the dispute. But in late August he signed a one-year "tender" offer worth $2.7 million as the two sides continued to talk about a longer-term deal.

But Levens wasn't the same, missing about half the season with a knee injury, yet another setback in a career pockmarked with them.

"My biggest hurdle was getting over the injury bug," he said. "I was just never able to do it."

The Packers championship window was also closing. After being eliminated in the first round of the playoffs by the 49ers (in which Levens rushed for a season-high 116 yards), Holmgren left to take the job as general manager and head coach of the Seattle Seahawks.

In 1999, he recaptured some of the magic, rushing for 1,034 yards and catching a career-best 71 passes. But injuries again plagued him and with each new problem, Levens pushed even harder to get back.

"The more I got hurt, the more I pressed to get back on the field," he said. "Sometimes, I pushed too hard."

In 2000, he played only a handful of games due to knee and ankle injuries. In his career, he was plagued by injuries that included everything from shoulders, to a hand to an assortment of knee and ankle issues.

Ironically, he played nearly the entire 2001 season, managing to stay as healthy as he ever was. But he was not the same back anymore and after that season, he was released.

"I still consider myself a Packer and most people remember me for that," Levens said. "But it was time to go and I thought a fresh start would motivate me. And it did."

In 2002, he signed with the Philadelphia Eagles as a backup but he knew even then that his days as an NFL back were coming to an end.

"My last season in Philly, I knew it was time," he said. "I remember thinking that everybody's just way too fast now. Here is a sadness when you realize that but my prime was three years before. Here was a sadness that I couldn't play at that high level anymore. But I played eleven years in the NFL where the average career is three and a half years. So I can't complain."

He just hopes that lengthy career in which he was the subject of innumerable collisions hasn't done permanent damage.

Since leaving the NFL, Levens has worked with youth groups and helped train athletes around the Atlanta area. But by far his greatest interest has come from working in the film industry, as a writer, director and actor. He's had bit parts before, including as an opposing coach in the movie *We Are Marshall*. He also filmed a movie in England titled *Gridiron UK*.

It was in 2012, though, when Levens found what may have been his calling—informing the public and other athletes about the dangers of concussions and how it impacts former players and their families. He was a writer and consultant on a documentary titled *Bell Rung* and it opened his eyes to what he felt was becoming a major issue in the sport he loves.

Perhaps the most dramatic evidence for Levens was meeting former New England Patriots and Philadelphia Eagles running back Kevin Turner, who in 2010 was diagnosed with amyo-trophic lateral sclerosis (also known as "Lou Gehrig's disease") at age forty-one.

There is a growing number of doctors who believe the colli-sions from football over the years can lead to chronic traumatic encephalopathy, a slow degeneration of the brain. Several former players, including Hall of Fame center Mike Webster and line-backer Junior Seau, were diagnosed with it after their premature deaths and several other players have committed suicide.

The NFL insists it is a small sample and it is taking steps to alleviate concussions. But Levens was a vocal critic two years ago when the NFL reached a $765 million settlement with the more than 4,500 plaintiffs (of which Levens was one) who claimed the NFL had knowledge of the effects of concussions and had covered it up.

"This is a great victory for them," Levens told the *Milwaukee Journal Sentinel* at the time. "I didn't understand how they got off so lightly."

But he intends to find out by keeping up the public awareness.

He admits he's also thought about coaching and does some on the youth level. But he's not interested, at least not these days, of moving on to another level. "I'm not really that interested because of the hours involved," he said. "I talked to [Packers running backs coach] Edgar Bennett and he said Mondays and Tuesdays are light days—only sixteen—and the heavy days were eighteen hours."

He remembers during his days playing when they'd have to gather for meetings during training camp.

"Some of those were just so exhausting," Levens said. "So in the running backs meeting, we'd all try to position ourselves so [coach] Harry Sydney couldn't really see what we were doing.

We'd put our hands over our eyes and looked like we were paying attention but we were sleeping. We were all sleeping."

He laughs at the memory and realizes now that coaches probably deserved a little more respect. And maybe that's why the profession holds little appeal to him.

"There's just no job stability and it all depends on the general manager and who the coach is," he said.

Then he laughed.

"Now maybe if it was only fifty hours a week, or maybe sixty, I'd do it," he said. "But I don't see that happening."

HARRY SYDNEY

"We had to change the culture."

HARRY SYDNEY

Position: Fullback. Ht: 6'0" Wt: 217

Born: June 26, 1959. Packers career: Played 1992, running backs coach 1995–99.

Career Highlights: Signed as a free agent by the San Francisco 49ers in 1987 . . . Started 10 of 16 games for Packers . . . Caught 49 passes and rushed for 163 yards . . . Wore No. 42.

Perhaps no one appreciated his NFL career more than Harry Sydney. That's because, perhaps, no one took such a circuitous route.

"Remember, I didn't make it to the NFL until I was twenty-seven," he said. "I'd been all over the place."

And maybe because nothing was guaranteed to him, Sydney embraced every aspect of the experience. And in many ways, he still does today.

He sees opportunities where few others do and isn't shy about letting others know about them. Because, as he knows only too well, the chances don't come often and you better grab them when they present themselves.

The burly, rugged fullback only played one season for the Packers, but it was in that pivotal 1992 season when the new regime of head coach Mike Holmgren came in.

Holmgren, who had come to Green Bay after a successful stint as quarterbacks coach/offensive coordinator with the San Francisco 49ers, wanted someone who understood the offense almost as well as he did. More important, he needed players he could trust who thought as he did.

"My job was to help the guys learn how to win," he said. "They didn't know. We had to change the culture."

But while he only played that single season, his impact could be felt throughout the organization and remained as he became a Packers' assistant coach and, eventually, settled in Green Bay and opened a non-profit organization called "My Brother's Keeper," a self-help mentoring group for men that he's run since 2003.

"Our society does a great job of taking care of women, animals and kids," he said. "But what about men? What are we doing for men? So I decided when I left coaching it was more important to coach boys and men. We help boys and men stay out of their own way. We help guys slow down and look at the big picture."

And there's nobody who's better looking at the big picture than Harry Sydney—he's been doing it his entire life.

He came from a difficult childhood of his own in Petersburg, Virginia, and found solace in football.

After a superb college career as a quarterback and then running back at the University of Kansas, Sydney was cut by both the Seattle Seahawks and Cincinnati Bengals. He then played in the Canadian Football League before going to the ill-fated United States Football League, where he was the leading rusher for the Denver Gold for two seasons and then signed with the Memphis Showboats before the league collapsed.

Sydney then took a job as a forklift operator and sent letters to every NFL team seeking a chance to show what he could do.

Only one team, the 49ers, contacted him, and he grabbed the opportunity with relish, serving as a special teams demon, running the ball on occasion and, most importantly soaking up an offense that would become a staple of the NFL for years to come.

He played five seasons in San Francisco, rushing for barely 600 yards in that time and catching 35 passes in limited offensive roles. But he saw an organization operating at the peak of efficiency, an organization that knew how to win and, more to the point, expected to win. He was part of back-to-back Super Bowl champions, winning the first in an epic last-second rally over the Cincinnati Bengals and the second in a thunderous rout of the Denver Broncos.

The 49ers, under head coach Bill Walsh, were the gold standard of the NFL and Sydney never forgot any of it.

He played two more seasons for the Niners and was waived during the 1992 training camp. But he wasn't quite finished yet—he had a 49ers alumnus anxious to scoop him up. Mike Holmgren was in his first training camp as head coach of the Packers and, after years of mediocrity, he was desperate for the kind of players who knew what it took to get the job done.

"Mike had told me that if I got through waivers that he was going to grab me," Sydney said.

And so it happened and Sydney joined the Packers just prior to the season opener. But neither Holmgren nor Sydney was concerned since the player knew the offense almost as well as the coach.

"Gil Haskell was the offensive coordinator and he knew the West Coast offense for about six months," Sydney said. "I knew it for five years. Guys would ask me questions about the offense all the time and I'd be happy to answer them."

Sydney was never under any illusions about his playing ability. He knew he was a functional fullback with an encyclopedic knowledge of the offense.

So in 1992, Sydney helped the young, evolving Packers team develop an understanding of the new system.

"I didn't see the pieces in place for a championship team that year," he said. "There was still so far to go. You had some of the things then it was a question of whether they'd buy into what Holmgren was doing."

Sydney played all 16 games that season, catching 49 passes, the third-most on the team. The Packers went 9–7 and barely missed the playoffs. Sydney saw that the Packers had a quarterback in young Brett Favre who, in time, could be pretty special.

Sydney laughs these days when recalling that season with the quarterback that no one knew anything about. It is well known in Packers lore that the first pass Favre completed was to himself. In the second game of the season, during mop-up duty in a loss at Tampa Bay, Favre was the backup to Don Majkowski and his pass was batted back into Favre's hands, who was tackled for a seven-yard loss.

"He was supposed to throw that pass to me," Sydney said.

Later that season, in a December victory over the Detroit Lions, Favre, now the undisputed starter, threw a nine-yard scoring pass to Sydney, making the fullback the only player in NFL history to catch touchdown passes from two of the game's all-time great quarterbacks, Favre and San Francisco's Joe Montana.

"I'm a Trivial Pursuit question," Sydney said with a laugh.

For Sydney, the season had provided for him exactly what he was looking for, a chance to teach the game to those who needed to learn it and to prove he still had plenty to offer as a player.

He had done his job superbly but the Packers had moved on and waived Sydney. The 49ers wanted to sign him the following season but Sydney knew it was time to move on.

"I said no," he said. "I told them no chasing anything anymore and I didn't want to be the weak link in the chain. I came out of college in 1981 and the only thing I wanted to do was start in the NFL. And I did that in Green Bay."

Sydney went on to do radio color commentary for a year. Then his former coach with the 49ers, Bill Walsh, suggested he look into becoming a coach. It was an idea that had intrigued Sydney for a while anyway.

"I wasn't as fast as everyone else so I had to be a student of the game," he said. "I always saw myself as kind of a player/coach anyway."

He had also broached the idea with Holmgren, and in 1994 he became the Packers assistant special teams coach, and in 1995 he took over as running backs coach.

He held the position through the 1999 season, helping lead the Packers to two Super Bowls in 1996–97. When Holmgren left after the 1998 season, he was retained by the new coach, and another old friend, Ray Rhodes.

But the Packers sputtered that year, missing the playoffs for the first time in six years. Rhodes and his entire staff, including Sydney, were fired. Even today, it stings.

"So many people didn't understand why Ray got fired," Sydney said. "He became a scapegoat unfairly. But it just shows you never wanted to be the guy who replaced a legend—and that was Ray."

Asked if he was interested in ever returning to coaching, he said simply, "No. I'm done. I have no desire."

That's because he has another desire—one that transcends everything he did on the football field. He had bigger concerns.

He knew that Green Bay was different from most NFL teams on many levels—including the fact there was an almost non-existent African American community.

For years, especially since Ron Wolf took over as general manager, the Packers had done an excellent job helping African American players feel comfortable, if not exactly at home, in a community like Green Bay.

As a black man, Sydney understood this all too well.

"I realized Green Bay is the American dream when you're old enough to know what the American dream is," Sydney said. "But the best and worst thing to happen to Green Bay was winning the Super Bowl [in 1996]. It wasn't Mayberry anymore."

But Sydney has made Green Bay his home with his wife and blended eight children. Working with local correctional facilities in the Green Bay area, Sydney works with men from ages seventeen to sixty-five to help them stay on the straight and narrow.

And while Green Bay seems to be a typical Midwest American city without the social issues of bigger cities, Sydney insists there are plenty of issues percolating just below the surface.

"I know the pulse and beat of Green Bay," he said. "I know the streets and I know the people. I also do 95 percent of the mentoring."

He works directly with boys and men who have a history of making bad decisions and teaches the concept of respect and responsibility.

He recalls an African American family that was unhappy with how a local school district was handling the discipline of their child.

"They said, 'There are no black teachers here,'" Sydney said. "So I ask them, 'Why did you move here?' and they said to get away from crime. So I said, 'Why would you bring that stuff up here?' People have to think about what they're doing and what's important to them."

Sydney said since opening My Brother's Keeper, he has conducted more than 20,000 sessions for boys and men to learn how to live better, and smarter, lives.

"We have a lot of success stories," he said. "We have examples of men going to college, going into ministries, they love their wives. They've really turned their lives around. It's unbelievable when you see it. My goal is to put domestic violence shelters out of business."

PAUL HORNUNG

"It's been fun being me."

PAUL HORNUNG

Position: Running back/kicker. Ht: 6'1" Wt: 215

Born: December 23, 1935. Packers career: 1957–66.

Career Highlights: *First-round pick of Packers in 1957 from Notre Dame . . . Inducted into Pro Football Hall of Fame in 1986 . . . Inducted into Packers Hall of Fame in 1975 . . . All Pro selection in 1960–61 . . . Pro Bowl selection in 1959–60; League MVP 1961 . . . Rushed for 3,711 yards, caught 130 passes and scored 72 touchdowns . . . Wore No. 5.*

For a fortunate few who played for the Green Bay Packers, there comes a point where the subtle transition is made. Most don't even know when it happens but, eventually, they understand that somewhere between walking off the field for the last time and settling into something resembling a life after football, you become what's come to be known all-too-commonly these days as an "icon."

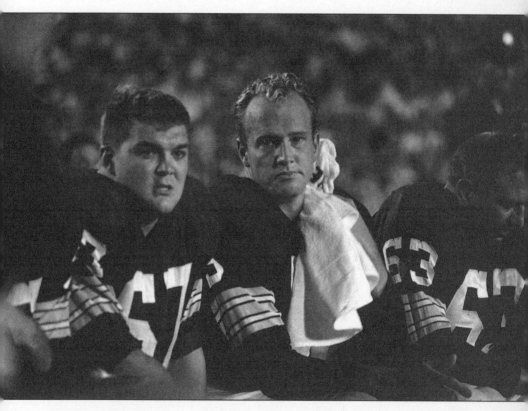

Paul Hornung takes a breather during an exhibition game on August 10, 1964—his first appearance after his suspension for gambling. With him are guards Dan Grimm (67) and Fuzzy Thurston. (AP Photo)

Many of those older Packers who played for Vince Lombardi are in that category now. They were part of those remarkable and legendary Packers teams that won five world titles in an eight-year period from 1960–67.

They had played for the great man, the coach who is still revered decades after his death. They played in a place that would come to be known as "Titletown," and they're the reason it got that name.

They put Green Bay, Wisconsin on the map and they have been a major part of keeping it there.

They had names like Bart Starr and Ray Nitschke and Dave Robinson and Willie Davis and Jerry Kramer and Herb Adderley.

And Paul Hornung.

They are part of that unique and shrinking fraternity of long-ago players who now make their lives being professional Packers. They can be found anywhere and everywhere, at golf outings and fishing tournaments and banquets and award ceremonies. They are the guys who regale longtime fans and those new to the faith with the stories of teams that were bigger than life.

The talk about the Ice Bowl and winning the first two championship games against the upstart AFL and the shock of Lombardi's departure and the sadness of his death barely two years later. They talk about great rivals like Norm Van Brocklin and Jim Brown and Dick Butkus. And they talk about what it was like to play for the greatest dynasty in NFL history in the greatest city in the league.

It's a great gig and no one plays the role better than the Packers perpetual bad boy, Paul Hornung.

"It's been fun being me," he said. "I think I've done a pretty good job of keeping my name in the public."

Indeed he has.

The Louisville, Kentucky, native has always enjoyed the good life and has always enjoyed the perks that have come from being the best in just about everything he did. And while he talks with a wicked smile about his exploits in such places as New York City and Miami and Hollywood and, his favorite city in the world, Chicago, his hometown has always been his home base. He still lives there, still works there, still counts it as the place where he developed and grew and where he cares most about what people think about him.

He is mostly retired now, though he still maintains office hours from his longtime office in downtown Louisville. He has succeeded in most of the business ventures he delved into, and it made him rich.

But in many ways, he's still just the son of Loretta, the woman he adored and still misses to this day.

"She was my biggest fan," he said.

And when he starred at Notre Dame in college, winning the Heisman Trophy in 1956, and then was the top draft pick of the Green Bay Packers in 1957, he was at the epicenter of one of the great turnarounds in pro football history.

And while it didn't happen overnight, it happened in the way it was supposed to happen—with smart drafting, the right scheme and putting the right players in position to do the job for which they were best suited.

That's part of what Lombardi did best. The other part was throwing the fear of God into them that, if they didn't play the way he demanded, he would damn well find someone who would.

Unlike many of his teammates, Hornung was never in awe of Lombardi, who became head coach in 1959 to find some way to turn a disastrous franchise around.

He had played in the NFL two seasons and had precious little to show for it. His first coach, Lisle Blackbourn, didn't like

Hornung and refused to take advantage of his abilities. His second coach, Ray McLean, whom Hornung viewed as a nice guy who was hopelessly overmatched in the NFL, didn't know what to do with him.

But his third coach, Lombardi, knew he had a powerful weapon and planned to use him in any way he could.

"He said to me, 'You're going to be my left halfback and if you can't play halfback you're not going to be in the league,'" he said.

Hornung reported to training camp in 1959 in the best shape of his life, committed to making it work in Green Bay and proving to the new coach, his teammates and fans that he was the player he always knew he could be.

"I could tell almost immediately that changes were coming because Lombardi knew exactly where I belonged in offense," Hornung recalled. "There was no question and no doubt and if it didn't work out, it was either because I didn't work hard enough or he didn't coach me well enough. That was exciting. I just wanted to play. I loved competition."

From the day Lombardi first stepped on the field, nothing was the same.

In his first game as head coach, the Packers beat their ancient rival the Chicago Bears, 9–6, on the way to a 7–5 record, Green Bay's first winning record since 1947. The Packers wouldn't see another losing season until 1968, the first one after Lombardi.

In that 1959 season, Hornung was a different player, rushing for a team-high 681 yards and seven touchdowns, both numbers which surpassed his first two seasons combined with the Packers.

By 1960, he was at the top of his game, as were the Packers. With his running, receiving and kicking, Hornung led the league in scoring with 176 points. The following season, he scored another 146 points, rushed for nearly 600 yards, caught 15 passes, kicked 15 field goals and was named the league's most valuable player.

He was an All Pro in both 1960 and 1961 and he was part of the reason the Packers went to the NFL Championship Game both years, losing to the Philadelphia Eagles the first year and beating the New York Giants the next year. Another title came in 1962 with another win over the Giants.

But even as he was enjoying success on the field, Hornung was also a part of that generation of players who had just as much fun off the field, and he wonders even to this day if some of that extra-curricular activity kept him from being an even better player than he was.

In the offseason, which in those days really did mean the offseason, Hornung could be found hob-nobbing with movie stars and fellow athletes in bars and restaurants from Los Angeles to Miami. He had numerous product endorsements including Chevrolet and Marlboro cigarettes and he loved to gamble.

"It was always just for fun," he said. "It was never about the money for me. I just enjoyed it."

But there was nothing fun about it in the view of NFL commissioner Pete Rozelle, who saw gambling as a growing problem, especially with rumors that organized crime was getting involved in it.

Hornung had placed his share of bets over the years through a good friend, Barney Shapiro in Las Vegas, and it had been, at least in Hornung's view, innocent enough.

"He'd put bets down for me and it was usually no more than seven or eight games a year," said Hornung, who maintained he never bet against the Packers. "I never had to. Remember, we were pretty good then."

But in the winter of 1963, at the peak of his career, Hornung was called to a secret meeting in New York with Rozelle, who asked bluntly if Hornung had been betting on NFL games. Hornung said no.

That was a mistake. The NFL, which had seen the growth of its league skyrocket, was sensitive to any negative publicity and unsavory perception. Officials had bugged Hornung's home phone and knew in fact he was gambling.

In April, Rozelle handed down indefinite suspensions for Hornung and Detroit Lions' defensive end Alex Karras for gambling.

Hornung admitted he had no defense but couldn't figure out what he'd done that was so awful.

"There was gambling going throughout the league," he said. "A lot of guys were doing it. But I took my medicine."

He missed the entire 1963 season but was reinstated the following year after promising to stay away from gamblers.

"I kept my nose clean," he said. "It wasn't hard because it wasn't like I was addicted to it. It was just fun."

But he wasn't the same player upon his return. He had worked in the offseason and came to training camp in the best shape of his life. But Jim Taylor was now the Packers No. 1 running back and Hornung was relegated to a secondary role.

As well, injuries began to catch up to him, especially to his knees. It got so bad, he could no longer kick field goals or extra points, forcing the Packers to sign Don Chandler, who had kicked the previous eight seasons with the Giants.

"I was in the training room a lot that year and I think that bothered Lombardi," Hornung said. "I don't know if he thought I was getting soft or what. But I was pretty beat up that year and I was beginning to feel it."

He had a good season in 1965, highlighted by a five-touch-down performance in a key Western Division battle with the Baltimore Colts.

But his knee problems, and now a troublesome neck injury, were beginning to hamper Hornung as well. He was unable to play in the first NFL-AFL title game (renamed the Super Bowl a couple of years later) in 1966 because of the neck injury.

"I remember Lombardi asked me late in the game if I wanted to go in just to say I'd be in it," Horning said. "I said, 'No, coach, I really don't.' He was OK with that."

And while no one knew it at the time, Hornung's NFL career was done. In 1967, he was left unprotected by the Packers and selected by the expansion New Orleans Saints.

"Lombardi was really pissed that I was taken but I think it was for the best," Hornung said. "I thought I could really help them."

But at the Saints' first training camp in San Diego, Hornung was concerned about the numbness he was feeling in his arms.

"I knew something wasn't right," he said.

He was checked by a doctor in San Diego, who was stunned by what he saw in Hornung's X-ray. Several of his vertebrae were no longer aligned with each other and the doctor offered this sobering warning: One more hit and you could be a paraplegic.

"That scared the hell out of me," Hornung said. "Nothing was worth getting paralyzed for. He suggested I retire right away and the next day, I did."

Fortunately for Hornung, he had set himself up nicely for life after football. He remained in New Orleans and did color commentary for Saints' radio and interspersed that over the years with TV analyst work on CBS and with his beloved Notre Dame.

He also was part of numerous business ventures, some of which he still maintains from his headquarters in Louisville. He has been involved in owning Kentucky Fried Chicken franchises throughout Kentucky and was co-owner of a distillery that he sold and made money on. He still holds several McDonald's leases in the Louisville area and he owns land in the west side of Louisville near his old high school that he hopes to develop.

A fan of horse racing for decades, he still owns several race horses and still has an eye, one day, toward getting one of his horses in the Kentucky Derby, an event he has religiously attended for years.

"One day," he says with a wry smile.

But mostly, he's in the business of being Paul Hornung.

He's involved in the Sister Visitor program, which helps at-risk girls, and he's still deeply involved with the award that bears his name, the Paul Hornung Award, started in 2010 through the Louisville Sports Commission and presented annually to the most versatile player in major college football.

"That means so much to me," he said.

As for his days with the Packers, he says they remain most special and fulfilling in a life of special and fulfilling moments.

He says he doesn't look back in regret on anything he did, or didn't do.

"I did what I did and I was happy about that," he said. "I don't think about it in any other terms."

He still gets back to Wisconsin in general and Green Bay in particular often and he still feeds off the adulation of Packers fans, many of whom these days weren't even born when he last played.

"It was the best place to play football," he said. "Sure, sometimes you wish you didn't have to deal with all that celebrity that comes with it. Still, it's pretty nice being Paul Hornung."

LYNN DICKEY

"I can't imagine . . . not having played with the Packers."

LYNN DICKEY

Position: Quarterback. Ht: 6'3" Wt: 215.

Born: October 19, 1949. Packers career: 1976–85.

Career Highlights: Third-round draft pick of Houston Oilers in 1971 . . . Traded to Packers in 1976 . . . Threw for 21,369 yards (fourth in team history through 2014) and 133 touchdowns . . . All Pro selection in 1983 . . . Inducted into Packers Hall of Fame in 1992 . . . Wore No. 10.

These days, Lynn Dickey's name doesn't reverberate through the state of Kansas as it once did. And that's OK with the former Houston Oilers and Green Bay Packers quarterback. After all, time moves on.

"Some of the people I deal with are forty-five years old," said Dickey, who works for Serve You, a Pharmacy Benefit Management company in Leawood, Kansas. "They have no idea who I am and that's fine. But if they want to hear old stories, I'll

Lynn Dickey warms up during a workout in Green Bay, July 24, 1979. (AP Photo/Steve Pyle)

tell them. But a lot of my clients are women and they really have no idea who I was or what I did."

But Packers fans? They know. Oh, do they know.

In the late 1970s and into the 1980s, in fact, Lynn Dickey triggered one of the most entertaining offenses the NFL has ever seen. In another time and in another place, it was an offense that would have rolled into the playoffs and, given the right circumstances and a little luck, might have even propelled those Packers to a Super Bowl.

But it never quite worked out that way. Dickey reached the playoffs just once, in the strike-shortened 1982 season, where the Packers lost in the second round of the "tournament" to the Dallas Cowboys.

"It was fun," Dickey said of his nine-year career with the Packers. "We were competitive in most all of our games. But I'm here to tell you that you can't put up 30 points and give up 33 every week and hope to win consistently."

All these years later, Dickey, who retired in 1985, remains among the Packers all-time leaders in passing yardage, touchdowns, completion percentage and, yes, interceptions.

But what a time it was.

Dickey, a standout quarterback at Kansas State, was a third-round draft pick of the Houston Oilers in 1971 and struggled with injury and inconsistency through four years with the Oilers.

Frustrated and ready for a change, Dickey asked the Oilers for a trade.

"I requested a trade to the Denver Broncos because my good friend, Charley Johnson, was retiring [as quarterback]," Dickey said. "I knew they had a great defense and they ran the ball a lot and those were the two factors you needed to be a championship team."

But what Dickey wanted and what the Broncos needed were two different things.

"John Ralston was the Broncos' coach at the time and he had absolutely no interest in me," Dickey said.

But Packers' assistant coach and former Packers player Lew Carpenter was intrigued.

"He'd been a coach with the Oilers when I was there and now he was an assistant coach with the Packers," Dickey said. "He enlightened [head coach] Bart Starr about me and thought I was someone they should consider. He instigated the trade."

And at that stage, the Packers were beyond desperate for a quarterback.

Green Bay was still trying to dig out from the rubble of a disastrous 1974 trade in which the Packers gave up their first, second and third-round draft picks in 1975 and their first and third-round selections in 1976 to the Los Angeles Rams for aging quarterback John Hadl.

It was widely regarded as one of the worst trades in NFL history and certainly the worst in Packers' history. Hadl was awful.

In 1975, Hadl's second season with the Packers, he threw for just 2,095 yards, six touchdowns and a staggering 21 interceptions.

So a week before the 1976 draft, the disgruntled Dickey and the desperate Packers got together. Green Bay dealt Hadl and defensive back Ken Ellis, a fourth-round selection that year and a third-rounder in 1977, to the Oilers for Dickey.

"I'd never been to Green Bay but I knew Bart Starr was the head and I knew Zeke Bratkowski was the quarterbacks coach and those were two good guys to learn from," Dickey said.

Dickey laughs now at the memory of his first journey to Green Bay.

"It was April 1, 1976, and I landed at O'Hare Airport in Chicago and I got off the plane and the air hit me," he said. "I thought 'Wow, that's cold.' And it's April. So I get on the Packers' private plane to take me to Green Bay and we land and there's snow everywhere. We drive through town and at every stop sign I see these snowdrifts eight feet high and I think 'I'm not in Houston anymore.'"

He laughs again.

"Now I can't imagine looking back in my career and not having played with the Packers," he said. "To not be a part of that player fraternity and that tradition, that would have been a shame."

But it didn't start well for Dickey, who was all but handed the starting job in 1976. He threw for nearly 1,500 yards the first nine weeks of that season but a separated shoulder in the 20th game ended his season.

It only got worse in 1977 as he threw 14 interceptions and just five touchdown passes and then, on the last play of the ninth game of the season against the Rams, he suffered a severely broken leg. The injury was so bad and resulting recuperation so extensive, he missed the entire 1978 season.

Finally healthy in 1979, he found himself backing the 1978 starter, David Whitehurst, for most of the season. But Whitehurst did not distinguish himself and with three games left in the season, the frustrated Starr inserted Dickey.

In those three games, Dickey threw five touchdown passes and four interceptions which, incredibly, was the first time a Packers' quarterback had more touchdown passes than interceptions since 1968, when Starr was still the quarterback.

And though the Packers lost two of those three games, Starr saw a quarterback he could build an offense around. And for the next five years, the Packers would sink or swim with Dickey under center.

From 1980 to 1984, Dickey stayed relatively healthy and, with a wide receiver cast that included the likes of James Lofton, John Jefferson and Phil Epps, and tight end Paul Coffman, the Packers could almost move the ball at will.

"In that time, we didn't even throw the ball that much really," Dickey said. "We didn't run that many plays. It seemed whenever we got the ball, we scored."

In those five years, Dickey threw for 15,565 yards with 101 touchdowns and 102 interceptions. He led the Packers to the playoffs in 1982 and played well in Green Bay's first playoff win in fifteen years, a 41–16 rout of the St. Louis Cardinals, when he threw for 260 yards with four touchdowns. But in the second round, against the Cowboys, despite throwing for another 332 yards, he also served up three costly interceptions.

In 1983, it all came together offensively for Dickey and the Packers. He led the league in passing yardage with 4,458 yards, which through the 2014 season is still the second-most in team history; touchdown passes with 32; and interceptions with 29 (he remains tied with Brett Favre for the most in a season).

But that team finished 8–8 and, again, missed the playoffs, which finally cost Bart Starr his job as head coach.

Forrest Gregg took over but nothing really changed for Dickey and the Packers. Two more average seasons followed but by 1985, Dickey was beginning to break down physically. Injuries again began to creep in and while working out during the 1985 season, he seriously injured his back, forcing him eventually, to retire.

In a thirteen-year career in Houston and Green Bay, Dickey threw for 23,322 yards and 141 touchdowns, both of which rank among the top 85 all time in NFL history. His 179 interceptions? They still rank in the top 20.

But he has no regrets. He landed in the place he felt was best for him and he's happy how it turned out.

He still marvels these days at how far NFL players have come since his days.

"I was up at Lambeau Field and now they have a full service restaurant in the players' area," he said with a laugh. "It's incredible. When I was playing we would hand in our dirty socks and jocks and our undergarments on Wednesday and there'd be a clipboard with an Arby's menu. We'd check off what we wanted and the trainer would pick out lunch for us. They do that on Thursday, too. And if we didn't pay them on Friday for the food, we wouldn't get our clean socks and jocks and stuff. Things have changed a little."

When his career ended suddenly in 1985, Dickey admits he wasn't sure what to do next.

"When I was playing I didn't have a real good idea what I was going to do once I retired," he said. "I thought I might get into coaching but then I saw more and more what they did. Coaches would get in at seven in the morning and not leave until midnight. I thought, 'Oh man.' I wasn't mentally ready to make that commitment. And the longer you're out of the game, the harder it is to get back into it."

Besides, Dickey had given all he could to the game.

"I did think about getting into it but I wanted to play golf and I wanted to go hunting," he said. "I wanted to enjoy my life. You've got to do what you've got to do to get ready for a season and I did that."

Dickey did go into several lines of work once he left the game, including selling extended auto warranties. But he's been with

Serve You for almost a decade now and it affords him the opportunity to work from home in suburban Kansas City while traveling the state.

And he admits on occasion he still thinks about his decision not to get into coaching.

"In hindsight would I have done it? I probably would have," he said. "But I don't wake up in the middle of the night wondering what would have happened. I have no regrets at all."

PAUL COFFMAN

"It was a dream come true."

PAUL COFFMAN

Position: Tight end. Ht: 6'2" Wt: 225

Born: March 29, 1956. Packers career: 1978–85

Career Highlights: *Signed as a free agent by Packers out of Kansas State in 1978 . . . Started 102 of 119 games for Packers . . . Caught 322 passes for 4,223 yards and 39 touchdowns . . . Pro Bowl selection in 1982, 1983, 1984 . . . Inducted into Packers Hall of Fame in 1994 . . . Wore No. 82.*

For Paul Coffman, there will always be something magical and lyrical and almost romantic about the game of football. It has always been that way with him because football gave him an opportunity he likely never would have gotten otherwise.

A farm kid from a small town in Kansas who played college football at Kansas State in what he called "arguably the worst college program in the country," Coffman nonetheless made the most of the opportunity.

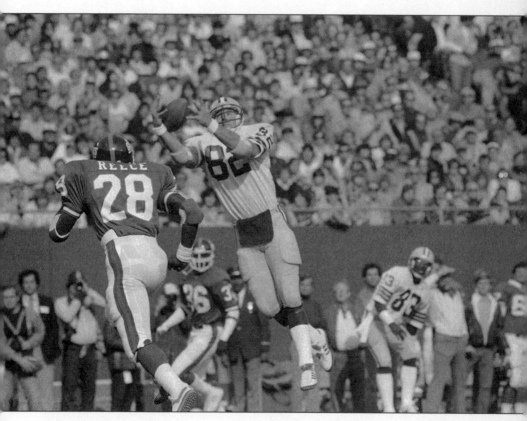

Paul Coffman playing against the Giants on October 5, 1981. (AP Photo/G. Paul Burnett)

He would eventually sign as a free agent with the Green Bay Packers and go on to a wonderful career in which he played eleven seasons, the first eight in Green Bay, where he would be named to three Pro Bowls and earn a spot in the Packers Hall of Fame.

To his mind, football has been everything. All three of his sons—Chase, Carson, and Cameron—have enjoyed football success of their own at both the professional and college level, and it hurts Coffman to his core to see the current attack on the game he loves.

He hears the criticism and the concern about concussions and brain injuries and whether the game is growing too dangerous for kids to play. He hears about how parents won't let their boys play anymore and he hears, incredibly, that some people think that football will not be part of the American landscape in another thirty years.

He doesn't believe it. He can't believe it. He won't believe it.

"There's risk and reward to everything," he said. "If you don't want your kids to get hurt, don't let them go outside. They could get hurt riding their bikes. It's gotten out of control. Football doesn't teach them to be violent, it teaches them structure. But it seems to be cool now to bash football players."

He continued.

"Football players are part of society," he said. "We are you. We're not all a bunch of morons. Football has been a big part of our lives. Football opens doors."

It certainly did for Coffman, who, almost by chance, got the opportunity to play in the NFL.

It began in 1978 when Coffman, a senior at Kansas State who had planned to use his agriculture degree to take back to farming, went along with friend and teammate Gary Spani, who was working out for the Packers. Coffman asked Packers assistant coach John Meyer for a tryout too and Meyer was impressed with Coffman's athleticism and hands.

After the 1978 draft, Meyer remembered Coffman and the Packers signed him as a free agent.

By the 1979 season, Coffman had stepped in as the starting tight end and was a consistent and reliable threat over the next eight seasons.

"We moved the ball and we scored touchdowns," Coffman said. "It was fun."

Coffman remembers how he would work on his game every day because he never wanted to take anything for granted.

"Linebackers would also mug me on the line of scrimmage," he said. "I mean they'd just beat me up. So every day after practice I'd have [Packers' linebacker] John Dorsey work with me. I'd tell him, "Make it as hard as you can to stop me from getting off the line. That's what you had to do.""

And he did it pretty well. In seven seasons with the Packers, not including the strike-shortened 1982 season, Coffman never caught fewer than 42 passes and his career total of 322 receptions remains a record for Packers' tight ends.

But times change, and sometimes they change when you least expect it.

In 1985, Coffman had just come off another solid season, catching 49 passes for 666 yards and six touchdowns. But as a new season loomed, head coach Forrest Gregg met with Coffman.

"He said, 'We have two options,'" Coffman recalled. "We're either going to trade you to the Buffalo Bills or we're going to cut you and Kansas City said they'll pick you up.' I was stunned. I didn't want to go to Buffalo and since I was from Missouri I said go ahead and cut me. Then Forrest said, 'OK, we'll do that; now you can be Kansas City's problem.' Kansas City's problem? When was I a problem for the Packers? I'd never given the Packers a moment of trouble. That hurt."

It also illustrated all too graphically to Coffman how quickly a career in the NFL can change.

"When you're playing, you never think it's going to end," he said. "Then this happens and they're telling you can't do it anymore. But I think I can."

Coffman went on to play two seasons as a backup in Kansas City and then moved on to the Minnesota Vikings in 1988 where he lasted eight games.

"A friend of mine said that last year in Minnesota that I was trying to muster something that wasn't there anymore," Coffman said. "It wasn't the eye of the tiger for me anymore. Football had my god."

And when it ended for Coffman, he wasn't sure what he wanted to do next, though he had ideas that it likely might involve the agriculture degree he'd earned at Kansas State. He even bought eighty acres of land and planned to settle in as a farmer.

Instead, a friend of his, Russ Meyer, kept trying to recruit him for the company he owned in Blue Springs, Missouri, Meyer Labs, which made chemical cleaners.

It wasn't exactly what he was seeking.

"I told him I didn't want to sell toilet bowl cleaners," Coffman said. "But Russ said, 'Think of all the repeat business.'"

So Coffman has been a salesman for Meyer, traveling around the state selling different chemical products to school districts, nursing homes, and businesses.

"But what I'm selling is me," he said. "If they like me, they're going to like my product."

He also spends time as a motivational speaker, youth coach, and extolling the wonders of what he still believes is the greatest sport on earth.

"Nothing you do after that will even simulate playing every Sunday in a NFL stadium," he said. "It lasted for me for eleven years and it was a dream come true and I gave it everything I had. Football is what you do, not who you are. I have value beyond football as a husband and father."

But he will never forget what a ride it was.

"I loved the game," he said. "Every Monday I got to practice. I got to run into people. And I got to do it at the highest level."

JAN STENERUD

"It's a special experience."

JAN STENERUD

Position: Kicker. Ht: 6'2" Wt: 185

Born: November 26, 1942. Packers career: 1980–83

Career Highlights: *Converted on 59 of 73 field goals with Packers . . . Scored 292 points . . . Signed as a free agent by Chiefs in 1967 and spent thirteen seasons with Kansas City . . . Inducted into Pro Football Hall of Fame and Packers Hall of Fame in 1991 . . . Named to NFL 1970s All Decade Team . . . Wore No. 10.*

In a nineteen-year Hall of Fame NFL career, Jan Stenerud's three and a half seasons in Green Bay might have seemed like little more than a blink of an eye.

But for Stenerud, coming to Green Bay after thirteen years with the Kansas City Chiefs was a lifeline, a chance to prove the doubters wrong and a chance to prove to himself that he was still one of the best kickers in the league.

It was also a chance to see just what football meant to the folks of a small community.

Jan Stenerud connects on a 36-yard field goal with one second left to beat the Los Angeles Rams, 27–24, on September 18, 1983. (AP Photo/Steve Pyle)

"What I remember most is the tremendous impact the Packers had on the community," Stenerud said. "It was important in Kansas City, but in Green Bay the situation was unique. The Packers are a huge part of people's lives. It's a special experience."

He got to see that firsthand starting late in the 1980 season and continuing through 1983. What he was able to do was bring stability to the Packers' kicking game, prove to himself and everyone else that he could still be a productive kicker and show that football careers don't necessarily have to end when you turn thirty.

"I knew I could compete with anyone in the league," Stenerud said.

Stenerud's story was one of the great tales of an NFL that was skyrocketing in popularity and taking the first steps toward becoming the international game it has ultimately proven to be.

A native of Norway, Stenerud came to the United States in 1964 on a ski jumping scholarship at Montana State University. One day, while training, he was kicking a football to an injured football player and his prowess caught the eye of the Montana State basketball coach, who then told the football coach.

He joined the football team the next fall and proceeded to kick a 59-yard field goal to beat rival Montana. Soon after, his scholarship was changed from ski jumping to football.

"I remember thinking back then, 'You can get a scholarship for kicking footballs?'" he said with a laugh.

He would go on to earn a spot in the NFL with the Kansas City Chiefs in 1967, and four years later, he was a key member of the Chiefs team that won the Super Bowl over the Minnesota Vikings.

He stayed with the Chiefs through the 1979 season, kicking 279 field goals and scoring 1,231 points, both statistics still No.

2 on the Chiefs' all-time scoring list. The irony, of course, is that No. 1 on the list is Nick Lowery, the guy who replaced Stenerud.

For years, Stenerud was upset at how he was cut loose by an organization for which he had done so much.

"Marv Levy comes in as coach and I was fifteen years older than my competition," Stenerud said. "I was the only player still on the roster from the Super Bowl IV team. So they released me in favor of Nick. I guess it made sense from that perspective but I was only thirty-nine years old and I knew I was still good enough. I was too young not to compete anymore. I was only two-thirds done with my career."

Meanwhile, the Packers were desperate to find some stability at the kicking position. Their longtime kicker Chester Marcol was struggling badly and was released in October of that season. He was replaced by Tom Birney, who missed 6 of 12 kicks in seven games. When Stenerud became available, they scooped him up.

He would go on to make 59 of 73 field goals over the next three seasons for a Packers team that he thought was close to contending for a title. He especially remembers the 1983 season, when he had five game-winning field goals to help the Packers post an 8–8 record.

But Bart Starr was fired after that season, a move Stenerud and many other Packers from that team still don't understand.

"We were close," Stenerud said. "I'm still convinced if Bart had gotten one more year he could've won a championship. We had a lot of injuries on defense that year and I think if we'd been healthy that next season we would have challenged for a championship."

It was not to be, though, and new head coach Forrest Gregg wanted to put his imprint on the team and made Stenerud part of the house-cleaning project, dealing him to the Minnesota Vikings.

"I had plenty of life left in me," he said. "I was only forty-two."

His job in Green Bay was handed to Eddie Garcia and he proceeded to miss six of nine field goals before he was replaced by Al Del Greco. The Packers field goal woes reached almost comical proportions in 1988 when four kickers—Max Zendejas, Dale Dawson, Dean Dorsey, and Curtis Burrow—all took turns trying to kick the ball through the uprights—and all failed. Between them, they made 13 of 25 field goals that season.

In the meantime, Stenerud moved on to the Vikings in 1984, hitting 20 of 23 field goals and earning a spot in the Pro Bowl. It was yet another chance for him to show yet another team that had given up on him that they had been premature in that assessment.

But as well as Stenerud kicked that first season in the Metrodome, even he began to realize that after years out-running time and age, he was going to eventually lose that race.

In 1985, he began to develop back problems that only got worse as the season progressed.

"It was also the first time in my career I had no one to compete against," he said.

But as his back worsened, his accuracy began to falter as well.

"I was just trying to finish the season standing up," he said. "The last couple of games I told [coach] Bud Grant that I just couldn't do it anymore. I was able to go as far as I could. I did not go out on my terms in Kansas City but I did in Minnesota. It was time."

For years afterward, Stenerud said he would run into his former Chiefs' coach, Marv Levy, at league meetings but would not talk to him.

"But years later, we buried the past," he said. "I enjoy his company."

Stenerud's remarkable career included four Pro Bowl selections, a spot in the Chiefs and Packers halls of fame, having his

No. 3 retired by the Chiefs, a spot on the NFL's 75th anniversary all-time team and his induction into the Pro Football Hall of Fame. His 1,699 points still ranks him among the top twenty scorers in NFL history.

Early in his career, Stenerud worked offseason at a bank and a local Kansas City TV station. He also developed a new kicking tee which he has sold commercially for years. In 1988, he started working for HNTB, a Kansas City architecture firm, where he was the director of business development.

One of the company's primary duties was to build and renovate sports stadiums. Among the projects was work on the 49ers new stadium as well as refurbishments of several Big Ten Conference stadiums including the University of Michigan, University of Iowa, Purdue University, and Michigan State.

"We wanted to do the work on Lambeau Field," he said with a laugh, "but we didn't get it."

He spent a number of years in Colorado but is now retired and is back in Kansas City where he enjoyed much of his professional success.

It was a career that came out of nowhere, but which has provided him with more than he could have hoped, and he acknowledges that Green Bay helped keep that career thriving.

"It was a great experience there and I still get up there a lot," he said. "My road from Norway to Canton, Ohio, was highly unexpected."

Where Have You Gone?

AHMAN GREEN

"I don't want the regret of not trying."

AHMAN GREEN

Position: Running back. Ht: 6'0" Wt: 220.

Born: February 16, 1977. Packers career: 2000–06 and 2009.

Career Highlights: *Traded to Packers in 2000 . . . Packers all-time leading rusher with 8,322 yards . . . Scored 54 rushing touchdowns and caught 350 passes for another 14 scores . . . Named to Pro Bowl in 2001, 2002, 2003, 2004 . . . NFC Player of the Year in 2003 . . . Inducted into Packers Hall of Fame in 2014. Wore No. 30.*

It's a pretty good list. There are names on there like Jim Taylor and Paul Hornung and Tony Canadeo and Clarke Hinkle and John Brockington. The first four names on that list? They're in the Pro Football Hall of Fame.

So Ahman Green doesn't take lightly the fact that he sits atop the list of all-time leading rushers for the storied and iconic franchise of the Green Bay Packers.

"To have my name on a list with those guys, that's very special," he said. "I knew when I got here I had to carry myself a certain way and I was up to the challenge."

Ahman Green takes off on a 31-yard touchdown run against Detroit on September 9, 2001. (AP Photo/Mike Roemer)

Indeed, when he got here, Green could see exactly what the challenge was. He had been a third-round draft pick of the Seattle Seahawks in 1998 but never saw significant playing time. In 2000, the Packers traded a fifth-round draft pick and corner-back Fred Vinson to the Seahawks for Green.

In the one-time University of Nebraska star the Packers saw someone who could re-ignite a running back that had started to sputter in recent seasons.

In the height of the Mile Holmgren years, Dorsey Levens had developed into a quality back. But injuries and time had reduced his effectiveness and other options, including one-time Chicago Bears' star Raymont Harris, had not worked out.

General manager Ron Wolf saw it was time to make a major commitment to the running game and Green seemed like the ideal option.

"I didn't know it was coming at first," Green said of the trade. "It was nothing I expected. But once I got here it was a blessing in disguise. I realized it was a place I probably should have been in long ago."

Green took over as the top tailback from the injured Levens and, after a slow start, rushed for 1,157 yards and caught 73 passes his first season.

That would be the first of five straight 1,000-yard rushing seasons for Green, including a single-season club record of 1,883 yards in 2003, In fact, of the Packers top 10 single-season rush-ing performances through 2014, Green owns four of them.

But while Green enjoyed individual success, the goal of getting back to the Super Bowl remained elusive. There were certainly close calls, but it was never to be, and as the toll of hundreds of carries began to build up, Green's effectiveness waned.

He missed 11 games in 2005 with injuries but re-signed with the Packers for a one-year deal that offseason and returned for his sixth 1,000-yard season in seven years.

In February 2006, Green signed a four-year, $23 million free agent deal with the Houston Texans where he reunited with his old Packers head coach, Mike Sherman, who was now offensive coordinator for the Texans. In two seasons there, Green carved out 554 yards in spot duty before he was released.

In October 2009, Green re-signed with the Packers and in a game November 8 against the Tampa Bay Buccaneers, Green became the Packers' all-time leading rusher, eclipsing the mark set more than forty years ago by Taylor.

After the season, Green retired. But unlike many players for whom the cold and relative isolation of Green Bay was simply too much, Green thrived on it and has made it home.

"I've been here since I was traded," he said. "I feel at home. I'm happy and content here. It ended up being a no-brainer playing here."

For Green, that has a lot to do with his upbringing in two diametrically opposed places—first as a kid growing up in Omaha, Nebraska, and then moving later to Los Angeles. Both areas steeled him for what was to come in life.

"In Nebraska, it was a quiet home life and that was something I was used to," he said. "But I lived in kind of a tough area in Los Angeles so you needed to learn how to do certain things. You learn that and I just looked at it as a part of growing up."

He moved back to Nebraska and attended the University of Nebraska, and when he was traded to Green Bay it suited him perfectly.

"I knew I wanted to be in a area that was safe for myself and my kids," Green said of his time living in Green Bay. "It's a different feeling here."

Green decided he wanted to get into the media business after football and took classes at the local community college and did spot work on a local TV station. He also hosts a Packers pregame show.

"I decided I liked it," he said. "It's right up my alley. I get a chance to talk football all the time."

Green also kept his hand in the game by coaching at two local high schools—one in Green Bay and one in Milwaukee. And as he did that, he understood he wanted to help kids learn more about the game—both physically and mentally.

So in 2012, he bought into D1-Green Bay, a national franchise that focuses on training for young athletes. But more than that, Green said, it's a family facility too.

"This area needed it," Green said. "We're a little unique because it's for the family. We can train every athlete for their sport but we can also help mom and dad lose weight."

"The more the merrier," he said.

What convinced Green to join was the fact that a number of top-flight pro athletes are also part of the franchise in different areas across the country. They include athletes like Peyton Manning, Robert Griffin III, Carmelo Anthony, Philip Rivers, and LaDainian Tomlinson.

"It was a no-brainer when I learned about the franchise," he said. "This is something I'm good at doing."

And while the new facility takes up much of his time, there is always more Green wants to do.

He and his wife, Marie, have formed the Ahman Green Foundation with a special emphasis on Alzheimer's Disease research as well as helping out the March of Dimes, which focuses on healthy children.

"We just want to raise awareness of how these things can impact families," said Green, whose mother is dealing with the ravages of Alzheimer's. "We just want to do our part."

But he admits he's always looking to what's over the horizon.

He's hired a talent agent and returns frequently to Los Angeles as he pursues possible acting opportunities.

"I don't want to do the same thing every day," he said. "I don't ever not want to try something. I don't want the regret of not trying."

GILBERT BROWN

"For a guy like me, it's hard to tell people no."

GILBERT BROWN

Position: Nose tackle. Ht: 6'3" Wt: 350

Born: February 22, 1971. Packers career: 1993–99, 2001–03.

Career Highlights: *Third-round draft pick of Minnesota Vikings in 1993 . . . Signed by Packers . . . Recorded seven sacks . . . Played in 125 games . . . Inducted into Packers Hall of Fame in 2008 . . . Wore No. 93.*

G ilbert Brown still looks down at his right arm and remembers. He remembers the pain and the sacrifice and realization that, in his words, "I played a whole season with one arm."

It's that gladiator mentality, that desire to play despite an injury that would drive a normal person to their knees, that always drove Brown when he played nose tackle for the Green Bay Packers.

"This is a man's game," he said. "I look at that arm and I think about what I gave to the game."

Gilbert Brown takes a breather against the Vikings on November 17, 2002. (AP Photo/Paul Battaglia)

There are no regrets, no second thoughts, no bitterness—at least not toward the organization that gave him an opportunity.

"I look at the Green Bay Packers as a car and [then head coach Mike Sherman] was the driver," Brown said. "Now if a car runs you over do you get mad at the car or do you get mad at the driver?"

The point is made.

"I didn't say I was done with my career," he said. "Mike Sherman said I was done."

But Gilbert Brown, one of the most recognizable and entertaining players in Packers history, has made peace with the past and is focused on a future that includes working with his foundation and helping those who need it most.

"There are 144 organizations that go through my foundation," he said. "And they're all special. For a guy like me, it's hard to tell people no."

So he rarely does and that's why his foundation helps people in all areas, from empowerment to health care to fighting the stigma of bullying.

He knows his fame as a Packer known affectionately as "The Gravedigger" is a major reason why people seek help and advice, and Brown is only too happy to help.

"The fans are a driving part of anything," he said. "Without the fans, there's no team. So people begin to know you almost as a family member and you wish you were family. The Green Bay Packers are the state of Wisconsin and it grows beyond that to all over the world. You can go to Tokyo and see people wearing Packers hats."

Then he laughs.

"You don't see them wearing those purple Vikings hats," he said.

Brown, who splits his time between Green Bay and his hometown of Detroit, is still as recognizable now as he was when he played the thankless position of nose tackle for some of the best, and underrated, defenses in team history.

Brown was well known for his "gravedigger" routine after a big play and he was known for his generous girth which usually fluctuated from 340 pounds to, at least according to some reports, 400 pounds during his playing days. He scoffs at those reports but admits weight was always an issue, and he might have extended his career if he'd kept it more under control.

Still, for his size, he was remarkably graceful and quick and shed blocks beautifully.

"[Defensive coordinator] Fritz Shurmur understood it so well," Brown said. "He knew that defense started up front. If teams couldn't get off the line, the other positions were obsolete. I knew my position wasn't a glamorous position. My job was to stop the run and make the linebackers look good."

Brown was originally a third-round draft pick of the Minnesota Vikings in 1993 out of the University of Kansas, but he reported to training camp as a troublesome 355 pounds and was cut late in camp.

The Packers, who were then in their second season under coach Mike Holmgren, were desperate for defensive linemen and thought Brown might be an intriguing investment, so they picked him. He didn't play much that first season and knee and elbow injuries limited his time the following two seasons.

But in 1996, Brown was able to stay healthy all season and was a major force for the NFL's top defense. He was surrounded by defensive ends Sean Jones and Reggie White and fellow tackle Santana Dotson as well as a secondary that included veteran safeties Eugene Robinson and Leroy Butler.

And while much of the talk that Super Bowl–winning year was about MVP quarterback Brett Favre and an unstoppable offense, the key to the season may well have been that defense.

"I get mad because that defense does not get the respect it deserves," Brown said. "The offense got all the credit but we gave up only 19 touchdowns all season—19 touchdowns. I'd put that defense up against some of the best defenses in NFL history."

And Brown also had his best season, recording a remarkable 53 tackles from his nose tackle spot and becoming a fan favorite for his enthusiasm and effort.

During the season, he was also spotted at a local Burger King, ordering a Triple Whopper with extra cheese with everything on it (except pickles). It also became a sensation and Burger Kings throughout Wisconsin began serving it as a promotion, and sales were better than they probably should have been. But it involved Brown and that's all that was necessary.

Brown was instantly recognizable around town and around the state, and while there were times he wished he wasn't, he also realized he had a responsibility and he thrived on it.

"Everybody has bad days but you can't show them to fans because those first impressions are important," he said. "You don't want them thinking you're an asshole. Being a Packer you had to have a good day every day and that can hard if you don't know how to handle it. I knew how to handle it."

He also picked the ideal time to have the best season of his career as free agency loomed that offseason.

His unique ability as a run-stopper intrigued several teams but concerns (real or imagined) about his weight issues resulted in only one team, the Jacksonville Jaguars, making an offer. And it was a beauty: three years for $9 million.

Yet Brown's decision surprised the football world, and even some of his Packers' teammates—Brown took less money to stay where he was happiest. He signed a three-year deal for what amounted to about $1 million less than the Jaguars offered.

"It was a not a tough decision," he said. "I love the game of football and money meant nothing to me. Where else can you go out and beat up on somebody and not get in trouble?"

But what mattered more to him was how comfortable he felt in Green Bay and with the Packers.

"I remember always walking down the hallway at the facility and seeing those championship banners hanging there," he said. "It always made the hair on the back of my neck rise. It was all that tradition. Ain't no amount of money could change that. I made the right decision."

He was ready to help the Packers return to the Super Bowl and while injuries caught up to him again, he did return in time for Super Bowl XXXII, the shattering 31–24 loss to the Denver Broncos that Brown still remembers.

But unlike other players from that team who believed the '97 team was better than the 1996 team that won it all, Brown said there was no comparison.

"The '97 team had a few guys who filled in roles," he said. "The 1996 team, to me, that was the team to beat."

Brown remained a major cog in the Packers defense for the next two seasons but a knee injury in 2000 led to his release.

The move stunned him.

"I kind of played myself out because of my weight," he said. "But life has to go on."

Brown vowed to get back in the league, specifically with the Packers, and he underwent a major workout regimen in which he lost some 40 pounds.

He was down to 325 pounds and the Packers re-signed him in the spring of 2001.

"I got myself right and I got my job back," he said simply.

But in a preseason game, Brown ruptured a tendon in his right arm and instead of undergoing surgery and perhaps losing another season, he decided to play through it. And he played well, recording 14 tackles and a quarterback sack.

"I played with one arm that season," he said.

But after the season, he was again released and this time there would be no chance to come back.

"I didn't make that call," he said. "Mike Sherman made that call. It kind of devastated me. It took me awhile to get over that."

Brown thought about continuing his career elsewhere, but after so many years in Green Bay, he just couldn't imagine starting over.

And he admits that even after all these years, football remains a part of who he is.

"Absolutely it was tough," Brown said. "It's in your DNA. It's in your blood. People don't understand that when it's a hot, sunny day and the grass is just cut and you can smell it in your nose, you know it's time for training camp. And it's tough because I never said I was done."

In the years since, Brown has been a coach for Green Bay's arena football team and, with his love of cars, he fulfilled a long-time dream by becoming a partial owner of the Milwaukee Mile race track.

But mostly, he concentrates on the Gilbert Brown Foundation.

"I've learned from things and I've tried to help people," he said. "I wouldn't change anything in the world."

BLAISE WINTER

"I fight for everybody."

BLAISE WINTER

Position: Defensive tackle. Ht: 6'3" Wt: 265

Born: January 31, 1962. Packers career: 1988–90

Career Highlights: Second-round draft pick of the Indianapolis Colts in 1984 . . . Signed as a free agent by Packers . . . Recorded 108 tackles and seven quarterback sacks . . . Wore No. 68.

The phone had stopped ringing and Blaise Winter didn't know why.

He had made a career after football of giving motivational speeches, using himself as the greatest example he knew of what hard work, determination and never, ever taking no for an answer could accomplish.

He had been one of the lucky ones. When his NFL career ended in 1995 after being placed on injured reserve by the Buffalo Bills, Winter had moved almost seamlessly into a new venture—talking to groups about the importance of staying true to yourself and never giving up.

And what stories he had to tell.

He had grown up outside Syracuse, New York, and from the start he battled for acceptance and recognition. He had tumors in both ears that were removed but which still left him deaf in one ear. He was born with a cleft palate that made it difficult for him to talk and which was the source of unrelenting teasing from kids in school. He underwent numerous surgeries to correct physical problems and, to make things worse, in sixth grade, he was even placed in a class for the developmentally disabled and to this day he doesn't know why.

But Blaise Winter battled through it all.

He found his sanctuary in football, first in middle school and then in high school, where he developed into one of the area's top defensive linemen.

When he heard nothing from any college programs, he proceeded to hit the road, visiting colleges and hoping for a chance to walk on with a program.

He got that chance at Syracuse University, where he was named the team's MVP his senior season. His unrelenting enthusiasm and drive, as well as his ability to get to quarterbacks, caught the attention of the Indianapolis Colts, who made Winter their second-round draft pick in 1984.

It was a great story that continued when, after he was released by the Colts, he was picked up by the San Diego Chargers, who then traded him to the Green Bay Packers in 1988, where he found a home for four seasons and became a fan favorite.

Eventually the career ended and Winter went off to tell his story that resonated with so many people.

"There was an empty part of me and that was the football part," Winter said. "I loved the motivational stuff but football has been part of my life since I was in middle school."

The story was irresistible.

But in 2008, the interest in that story waned.

"That's when it flipped," Winter said. "I went from one hundred speaking engagements a year to twenty. The phone went from being busy to nothing. It was a complete washout. It was like the phone was broken. I told my wife that my motivational speaking career was done."

But in the world of Blaise Winter very few things are ever done.

He has reinvented and redefined himself and through the kind of struggles he's dealt with all too often, he has come out of the other side happy and as enthusiastic as ever.

His three seasons in Green Bay were among the happiest and fulfilling of his career, not only professionally but personally.

Playing out of position at nose tackle in '88, he recorded five sacks, second-best on the team that season. In 1989, he was defensive end and had two more sacks. But his effectiveness dropped off in 1990 as the Packers' fortunes took another nose dive and he was released in the spring of 1991.

But Winter had found a home in Wisconsin and he and his family stayed in Green Bay as Winter awaited the next phase. He assumed he'd be contacted by other teams in need of a defensive end whose motor never stopped running.

Instead, he heard nothing.

"I couldn't understand it," he said.

In January 1992, as he had done before in his life when he needed to sell what he had to offer, Winter struck off, driving around the country seeking an opportunity to show what he could do.

He recounts a story to the *Milwaukee Journal Sentinel* of how, while in Anaheim, California, talking with the Los Angeles

Rams, his car was broken into and everything was stolen. He offered to work out for the Rams in his underwear and bare feet.

His determination finally paid off when he was re-signed by the San Diego Chargers and, starting 31 of 32 games over a two-year span, he recorded a total of eight sacks. He missed most of the 1994 season with injuries but he still had a chance to be with the team in the Super Bowl loss to San Francisco.

He was released again and tried to catch on with the Buffalo Bills, but seventeen surgeries in a twelve-year period had worn him down, and when the Bills placed him on injured reserve, he retired.

He moved his family back to Appleton, Wisconsin, thirty minutes from Green Bay, where he and his wife raised their three kids. Winter moved on to motivational speaking.

But when that phase ended in 2008, he did what he's always done, he found a new direction. Winter had studied martial arts for years and, after encouragement from other coaches and players, was convinced to start a clinic to incorporate martial arts into football. He continues to do that.

"I teach football players and coaches how to fight better by using martial arts techniques," he said. "That's what football is. It's fighting and if they know the right way to do it, that can only help them."

But in 2012, he had a chance to try something else and it came in the form of a phone call from a man he had often called his "father figure."

George O'Leary, who had been Winter's defensive line coach at Syracuse, was now head coach at the University of Central Florida in Orlando.

"He called me and said, 'My defensive line coach is leaving and I'm giving you another chance. Do you want to coach?'" Winter recalled.

It was a move Winter wasn't sure he wanted to make. His family was established in Wisconsin and moving to Florida was a major decision.

"But my wife [Angie] said if you don't do this, it's something you'll always wonder about," he said.

So he moved the family to Orlando and after one season with his old coach, he quit.

"I had discovered what others had warned me about with George," Winter said. "I loved every part of working with the players but I hated the behavior of the head coach. I wasn't going to be abused by this man. He's a bully."

The two men locked horns frequently during the 2012 season and O'Leary finally offered Winter the opportunity to resign. He took it immediately.

"He was my position coach in college and I said to him, 'What's happened to you?'" Winter said.

Winter and his family still live in Orlando and his motivational speaking career, which he thought had run its course, is now back.

He admits he misses Wisconsin and the slower, easier life.

"My wife said that this is where faith comes full circle," Winter sad. "We're here for a reason."

From his base in Florida, he now travels the country, once again delivering his message of hope and determination. And, as always, he uses himself as his best example.

"I believe I am a purpose-driven human being," he said. "I have a hard time sleeping at night if I'm not empowering people. I didn't want to chase money, I wanted to chase opportunity and I've learned you don't just do something for money. I'm a fighter. I fight for everybody. I have no idea what I'm doing half the time but I love doing it."

GEORGE KOONCE

"I felt the game left me."

GEORGE KOONCE

Position: Linebacker. Ht: 6'1" Wt: 245

Born: October 15, 1968. Packers career: 1992–99

Career Highlights: *Signed by Packers as a free agent from World League of American Football . . . Started 102 of 112 games . . . Recorded 433 tackles, 7-and-a-half sacks and recovered 6 fumbles . . . Wore No. 53.*

Even when he was playing football, George Koonce was the kind of guy to think about what life would be like when football was over.

After all, he thought, it's fine to never take anything for granted, but you better have a plan in place when you find out you're right.

He learned that the hard way, growing up in knee-buckling poverty in a shack on a dirt road in North Carolina, that nothing was going to come easily, or quickly, to him.

George Koonce and George Teague (31) wrap up Blair Thomas in a game on January 8, 1995. (AP Photo/Tim Sharp)

So when he was able to attend East Carolina University and play football well enough to eventually be signed as a free agent by the Green Bay Packers in 1992, he knew the road could be as long, or as short, as he wanted to make it.

"Ninety-nine percent of players don't walk away from the game when they want to walk away from it," he said.

And he knows because, despite playing his first eight seasons for the Packers and one more for the Seattle Seahawks, and starting 125 of a possible 138 games as an NFL linebacker, the end comes to everyone.

It's those who know how to deal with it who can thrive and Koonce, after admittedly struggling with that reality at first, is at peace with life after leaving the game he still loves.

But he also says he keeps the game at a distance now.

"I know as a player, and with my personality, that I didn't want to be a coach," he said. "I had the chance but I didn't want to. I'd rather just see it from the sidelines. I'd rather just be a fan. I lived it so much that I'd like to leave it the way I remember it. I'm a huge fan and I don't want to get caught up in the analytics of it. It's a great sport."

Since 2014, Koonce has been the vice president of advancement at Marian University in Fond du Lac, Wisconsin. In that role, he deals with student engagement, strategic planning and philanthropic efforts to help raise money and awareness for the university.

"We want to try and help young people live out the American dream," he said.

Prior to that, he was athletic director at the University of Wisconsin-Milwaukee for a year; associate athletic director at Marquette University from 2007 to 2009 (where he also earned his PhD in sports management); director of player development for the Packers in 2006; and assistant athletic director of development at East Carolina from 2004 to 2006, where he gained his master's degree in sports management.

Administration has always been a passion of Koonce's, who'd discuss the topic in the locker room with teammates when he played and would keep an eye on Packers' front office leaders like general manager Ron Wolf for tips on how to run an organization.

"When we'd have conversations about what our careers would look like after football, for me it was always on the administrative side," Koonce said. "This has been part of my trajectory for the last twelve or thirteen years."

But it didn't come without hardship.

Koonce originally signed as a free agent with the Atlanta Falcons in 1991 and was quickly cut before latching on with the Ohio Glory of the World League of American Football, where he was the starting middle linebacker.

The Packers signed him in 1992, and he ended up starting 10 of 16 games as an outside linebacker for new coach Mike Holmgren.

Koonce would anchor the Packers linebacking corps through the 1999 season. He was part of the era that saw the Packers go to three straight NFC championship games and two Super Bowls.

And as successful as those teams were, Koonce wanted more.

"I have a lot of fond memories from those days," he said. "I just wish we could have won more games. We had some outstanding players like Reggie White and Sean Jones and Robert Brooks and Edgar Bennett and so many others. And not only that, they were good people. And we all came together as one."

But Koonce was released after the 1999 season and signed with the Seahawks, where he started sixteen games in 2000 before he was released.

He finished with 433 tackles in his Packers career and more than 500 overall in the NFL. And the collisions took their toll. But even though he suffered eleven concussions and seven surgeries, he found it hard to leave the game behind.

"I had a blast," he said. "I'd do it all over."

But when he was cut by the Seahawks, he suffered through the same feelings of rejection, frustration and depression as so many other players.

"I felt the game left me," he said. "I didn't have a chance to leave on my own terms and that made it more difficult to transition."

He recounted to the *New York Post* a few years ago that he was so despondent and unsure about his future that, while driving to the beach to clear his head, he accelerated his truck to seventy-five miles an hour, "Just to see what would happen."

The truck flipped over but Koonce was uninjured. It was then and there that he knew he could finally walk away from football too.

And it was just last year that Koonce teamed up with two sociology professors at Marquette University to write a book titled, *Is There Life After Football? Surviving the NFL.*

"It looks at the stumbling blocks NFL players face when they leave football," said Koonce, who put eight years of research into the project.

And while researching the book, he started seeing the disquieting statistics about concussions and chronic traumatic encephalopathy, which many observers see as a growing problem in professional sports, especially football.

CTE, many now believe, is a problem in the NFL and can lead to diseases such as Alzheimer's.

Koonce admits he's concerned because he can't even count the number of major collisions he had in the NFL.

"Most definitely it concerns me," said Koonce, who has kept track of his condition with trips to the Cleveland Clinic. "From the cognitive perspective I'm OK—for now."

He says he also suffers from herniated discs in his neck and back that make walking difficult. But he knew the risks when he signed up and he's okay with that.

"If I hadn't gotten a football scholarship I never would have gotten in to college and I was the first one in my family to go," he said. "Nobody, when I look at my situation, has had a better athletic career. I can't imagine doing anything else."

CHRIS JACKE

"You never want to leave a place you love."

CHRIS JACKE

Position: Kicker. Ht: 6'0" Wt: 205

Born: March 12, 1966. Packers career: 1989–96

Career Highlights: *Inducted into Packer Hall of Fame in 2013. . . . Sixth-round draft pick of the Packers in 1989 . . . Scored 820 points and made 77 percent of his field goals . . . Named All Pro in 1993 . . . Wore No. 13.*

In the summer of 2013, as he was being honored for his induction into the Green Bay Packers Hall of Fame, it dawned on Chris Jacke that being a Packers player was not something you did but something you were.

You were part of a fraternity, part of a family, part of a tradition like no other in the NFL and, perhaps, like no other in sports.

Somewhere deep inside, he probably knew that all along, even after he left Green Bay after eight highly productive and sometimes contentious seasons.

Chris Jacke hits a first-quarter field goal during Super Bowl XXXI.
(AP Photo/Mark Humphrey)

But when he joined the pantheon of Packers in the hall of fame that included names like Starr and Hornung and Nitschke and Lombardi and so many others, it hit Jacke like a football between the eyes: He was part of it.

And it gave him an idea.

"I was working in the financial industry and I wasn't getting up in the morning excited to do that," he said.

He knew that former Packers, including himself, were always in high demand around the region for everything from appearances at golf tournaments and fishing derbies to speaking at local chambers of commerce, businesses and schools.

So with the help of his wife Terri, an organizational development trainer, he set about moving forward with his idea to develop a website that would coordinate a network of former Packers who could be requested and contacted for events all over the area.

What was born was Player Alumni Resources, which Jacke runs out of Green Bay, where he's made his home for years. For him, it has been a chance to give back not only to teammates but to the fans who have remained devoted for so long.

More important, he's found exactly what he wants to do.

"I wasn't excited by what I was doing before," he said with a laugh. "Now I'm excited."

Jacke has corralled some fifty former Packers, most of whom played with him in Green Bay when he was the team's record-setting kicker from 1989 to 1996.

The website, playeralumniresources.com, provides those interested in hiring a Packers player with options of who and when they can appear and Jacke coordinates fees and dates.

"I just start brainstorming and was thinking about what it was that Wisconsin likes to do?" he said. "They love the Packers; they love golf, at least the three months out of the year they can play; and they love fishing."

So those are links to the website and Jacke is involved with making sure the players make it.

To sell the idea, Jacke spent the first seven months traveling the state, introducing himself to company presidents and human resources directors, who are the ones usually responsible for setting up corporate and company outings, conferences and meetings.

"I think people who go to these would like to hear a Packer, not a CEO," Jacke said. "It would be memorable. It wouldn't be dry."

Jacke said the response has been better than he could have hoped for and he said there are plans already in the works to expand the network to other Wisconsin sports such as the Milwaukee Brewers and Milwaukee Bucks and the University of Wisconsin.

For Jacke, celebrating the Packers and the state are natural since it's a place he's made home for years. Indeed, he never wanted to leave the Packers in the first place.

"You never want to leave a place you love," he said.

And it seemed that would never happen. After all, Jacke settled and solidified a kicking situation that had been a running joke in the late 1980s.

It really started when the Packers traded future Hall of Famer Jan Stenerud in 1984. For the next five years, there was little in the way of stability or quality with Packers kickers. It reached the point of utter absurdity in 1988, when the Packers tried four kickers through the course of the season and, between them, they couldn't make 50 percent of their kicks.

So in the 1989 draft, the team went against common wisdom and drafted a kicker, taking Jacke from the University of Texas–El Paso, in the sixth round.

"I knew they'd had problems in that area and there was a lot of pressure on because I was a draft pick," he said. "I think they had four or five guys in training camp but I think I had an advantage in that department because I had been drafted. But if any of the others had shown more, I wouldn't have made it. I was very fortunate. I think 98 percent of it was being in the right place at the right time."

Jacke would emerge as one of the unexpected stars of that remarkable 1989 season. He kicked three game-winning field goals—beating Atlanta, Detroit in overtime and then drilling a 47-yarder in the final seconds for an improbable win over Tampa Bay.

The Packers finished 10–6 that year, with ten of its sixteen games decided by four points or fewer. They were known as the "Cardiac Pack," and Jacke reveled in it.

"That season was a lot of fun," said Jacke, who made 22 of 28 kicks. "It seemed like it was something new every week. And the fans were just great. It was like a college atmosphere."

Jacke continued to kick well, but the Packers' fortunes turned sour over the next two seasons and head coach Lindy Infante was fired by new general manager Ron Wolf.

In stepped former San Francisco 49ers coordinator Mike Holmgren as coach and Jacke could immediately see changes.

"What I saw on the surface is that it was going to be run like a business," he said. "They literally changed everything that wasn't successful. What was really telling was the number of free agents they brought. They knew they had to. They were always looking to make the team better."

And in time, he saw a remarkable transformation.

"When I first got there Green Bay was a place no one really wanted to play," he said. "Players on other teams were threatened that if they didn't play better, they'd be traded to Green Bay. Ron and Mike made Green Bay a place people wanted to play."

Jacke was part of that renaissance in Green Bay, making 77 percent of his kicks and, over eight seasons, he scored 820, which then was second only to the iconic Don Hutson as the team's all-time leading scorer.

But after the Packers' Super Bowl–winning season, changes came and the Packers, amazingly, drafted Penn State kicker Brett Conway, in the third round of the draft. Jacke, whose contract had expired and who was experiencing hip problems, could see the writing on the wall.

"It does take you a while to realize that the NFL is a big business," he said. "You can't worry about it."

He signed a free agent deal with the Pittsburgh Steelers but never played a game because the hip injury worsened.

Meanwhile, Conway was hurt early in training camp and was replaced by an unheralded kicker from the University of California named Ryan Longwell, who would grab the job and hold it for the next nine seasons. He would take over as the Packers all-time leading scorer before his successor, Mason Crosby, would usurp him.

Jacke never played a game for the Steelers but was signed late that season by the Washington Redskins. The next year, he signed with the Arizona Cardinals, where he stayed for two seasons before retiring.

"I would have loved to have finished my career in Green Bay," he said. "But my body was basically breaking down. I've had back surgeries and ankle surgeries even since I retired."

Once he was done playing, he went back to Wisconsin to pursue a career in the financial planning industry before jumping into his new endeavor.

"Being a former athlete, you always want instant gratification," he said. "So is this growing as fast as I want it to? Probably not. But my wife, who's an expert in this field, says we're ahead of the curve and I believe her. We have our eyes on expansion and we think a lot of people are going to want to be a part of the most historic franchises in sports."

JAMES LOFTON

"The writing was pretty clear on the wall."

JAMES LOFTON

Position: Wide receiver. Ht: 6'3" Wt: 190

Born: July 5, 1956. Packers career: 1978–86

Career highlights: Inducted in Pro Football Hall of Fame (2003); Seven-time Pro Bowler (1978, 1980, 1981, 1982, 1983, 1984, 1985) . . . All-Rookie Team (1978); Member of NFL 1980s All Decade Team; Inducted into Packers Hall of Fame (1999) . . . First-round draft pick of the Packers in 1978 . . . Wore No. 80.

No one had to show James Lofton the door. It was wide open and he was ready to step through it.

"The writing was pretty clear on the wall," said the longtime NFL receiver, who played sixteen seasons, the first nine with the Packers. "It was time. I was a thirty-seven-year-old speed receiver who couldn't outrun anyone anymore."

No regrets, no recriminations, no bitterness, no looking back. For Lofton, it had been every bit the career he had hoped it would but never dreamed it would be.

Rookie James Lofton coasts into the end zone after catching his second of three touchdown passes, September 10, 1978. (AP Photo)

He even looks back with bemusement at his last season in 1993 when, in the course of one calendar year, he was on the roster of four teams.

"In January, I played with the Buffalo Bills," he said. "Then I was released and I was on the roster of the Raiders and then I played [nine games] with the Eagles and then [one game] with the Rams. Four teams in one year. That was pretty interesting."

It also showed him that his name, and ability, still carried some weight and that if he couldn't hook on with any of those teams that it might be time to move on.

So Lofton, who finished his career with 764 receptions for 14,004 yards (which at the time of his retirement was the most in NFL history), walked away from playing and into the next phase of his life.

For Lofton, it was a battle between coaching the game he knew and loved or broadcasting, a skill he also had.

In 1994, Lofton joined CNN as a pro football analyst and then went to NBC in 1997 before returning to CNN in 1998. From 1998 to 2001 he was a color analyst for Fox and also handled preseason color commentary for the Carolina Panthers from 1995 to 2001.

But coaching continued to tempt him and in 2002, he gave up his broadcasting duties when he was named wide receivers coach for the San Diego Chargers. In 2006, he got his opportunity to interview for a head coaching position—at his alma mater Stanford—but lost out to Jim Harbaugh.

He remained with the Chargers until after the 2007 season, when he was fired.

Later that year, he was a candidate for head coach of the Oakland Raiders but, again, didn't get it. Instead, the next year he was named the Raiders' wide receiver coach but was fired a year later with the rest of the staff.

He also was a candidate for the Buffalo Bills' head coaching job but it never came together. And looking back, Lofton is thankful it didn't.

"Going from a position coach to a head coach isn't always easy," he said. "I'm not sure if it would have worked out. I was fortunate to coach in the NFL because now I realize how hard it is to get a coaching job in the NFL."

But it also showed him that those days were over. Since 2009, he's been back in broadcasting, this time as sideline analyst for the Westwood One network's NFL coverage.

"I didn't want to get on the coaching treadmill," said Lofton, who lives in San Diego. "Broadcasting allows me to stay where I am. I love being on site. I still know enough players I coached and might have coached against so I like that. It's a fraternity. And the next best thing if you're not a player and not coaching is to be broadcasting."

Asked about possibly returning to coaching, Lofton laughs.

"That's a distant speck in the rear-view mirror," he said.

But he still fondly remembers his playing days with the Packers, when he was part of an offense that was among the most entertaining and exciting in the league.

He was Green Bay's top draft choice in 1978, the first election of new head coach, and former Packers legendary quarterback, Bart Starr. And he introduced himself to Packers fans in a thunderous fashion when, in the home opener, a 28–17 win over the New Orleans Saints, he caught three passes (all for touchdowns) for 107 yards.

He went on to make the league's all-rookie team with 46 receptions and six touchdowns. He would never miss a game in nine seasons and catch 530 passes (third all-time in team history) for 9,656 yards (still second in team history through the

2014 season). He also led the league in yards per catch average in 1983–84.

But his career in Green Bay did come to a shattering, and stunning, end when he was arrested and charged with second-degree sexual assault late in the 1986 season. The charge forced the Packers to hold him out of the season-finale, the first game he ever missed with the team.

And though he was found not guilty in a lurid and very public trial, the Packers, already in the midst of other public relations disasters, cut him loose. In April 1987, they traded him to the Los Angeles Raiders for a third- and fourth-round draft pick.

In two seasons with the Raiders, his numbers toppled and he was released after the 1988 season.

But Lofton was convinced he still had something to offer and he sent letters to several NFL teams seeking an opportunity for a tryout. Only one, the Philadelphia Eagles, responded, and they decided not to sign him. When a chance with the Bills opened up, though, Lofton grabbed it and he enjoyed a renaissance rarely seen in the NFL.

In four seasons with the Bills, Lofton caught 151 passes for more than 2,700 yards and in 1990, at age thirty-five, he caught 57 passes for 1,072 yards, making him the oldest player in league history at the time to break 1,000 yards receiving.

In 1999, all was forgiven with the Packers' organization and fans and he was inducted into the Packers Hall of Fame. Four years later, Canton, Ohio, came calling and he was placed in the Pro Football Hall of Fame.

"Your perspective changes on a lot of things," Lofton said of his time in Green Bay. "Obviously playing in the shadow of Vince Lombardi will always be very special to me. And as a former Packer you delight in the success they've enjoyed for—what?—the last fifteen years or so."

He is where he wants to be and doing what he wants to do right now and he couldn't ask for more.

"All of life is about evolving and adapting," he said.

CHUCK MERCEIN

"I was in the right place at the right time."

CHUCK MERCEIN

Position: Fullback. Ht: 6'2" Wt: 225

Born: April 9, 1943. Packers career: 1967–69.

Career highlights: Third-round draft pick of the New York Giants of the NFL in 1965 . . . 10th-round pick of the AFL's Buffalo Bills . . . Traded to Packers in 1967 . . . Key player on famous final drive of the 1967 "Ice Bowl" . . . Wore No. 30.

Two plays. In the final analysis, Chuck Mercein's Green Bay Packers career would be remembered best for two dramatic plays in one of the NFL's most iconic games.

"Fans have never forgotten," Mercein said. "And they never will."

Just say "Ice Bowl" and every football fan, whether rooting for the Packers or not, remembers something about it.

"I read somewhere that it was the most replayed game in TV history," Mercein said. "My kids say I pay NFL Films to replay it. They say I should get royalties."

Chuck Mercein is congratulated by Vince Lombardi after the Packers won their third successive NFL title, January 2, 1967, by beating the Cowboys, 21–17. (AP Photo/Paul Shane)

And all these years later, Mercein, the Milwaukee native and Yale University graduate who went on to a successful forty-year career on Wall Street, is proud that his contribution is still revered.

"It was an honor to be remembered by so many people," he said. "I was in the right place at the right time. That's what every player dreams of."

The game remains legendary all these decades later, and not just because of the horrific weather conditions and what was at stake. It was a study in survival by both teams: it was a team seemingly beaten and demoralized finding one more spark; and it proved to be the end of an era even though no one really knew it at the time.

The official crowd at the game was just over 40,000 fans, but the game has become such a part of local and NFL lore that, apparently, everybody in the state of Wisconsin was actually sitting in the stands claiming to have seen it.

Mercein laughs.

"I think I just met the 500,000th fan who was there," he said.

And why not? It was a game never to be forgotten.

The setting was Lambeau Field in Green Bay. The date was January 31, 1967. It was the NFL championship game between two bitter rivals—the Packers, the established power, and the rising stars to the south, the Dallas Cowboys.

Green Bay had beaten the host Cowboys the year before in the title game and moved on to blast the Kansas City Chiefs in the first NFL-AFL championship game (later to be known as the Super Bowl).

The two teams were meeting again in 1967, but this time in Green Bay. And by now everyone knows the story. A surprise arctic cold front rolled through Wisconsin the night before the game, sending temperatures plummeting below zero while kicking up a wind that sent the wind chill, a relatively new phrase even to hardy Wisconsinites, to minus 25.

Commissioner Pete Rozelle briefly considered postponing the game but decided against it. He might not have made that decision if he had known the state-of-the-art electrical coil system Packers coach Vince Lombardi had installed that season to keep the field warm had malfunctioned due to the cold.

So instead of a warm turf field, it was a hard layer of ice and neither team could get traction the entire game. And it got progressively worse as the day wore on and it got darker and colder.

It wasn't so much a football game as a battle between two desperate teams seeking only to get out in one piece while, somehow, coming out with a victory that would send them to the world championship.

The Cowboys were ready to take their place as the NFL's next powerhouse, but first they had to dispense with the Packers, who had won four NFL titles in the previous six seasons.

And they were ripe for the taking on this frigid Sunday.

The Packers dynasty was nearing its end. And while injury and age had taken its toll, these Packers were not done just yet. Not as long as Bart Starr was the quarterback and not as long as Vince Lombardi was the head coach.

And into this maelstrom came Chuck Mercein, a talented back in his own right who had worn out his welcome with the team that had drafted him, the New York Giants.

"Allie Sherman [the Giants' coach] and I had never saw eye to eye," Mercein recalled.

He had been a member of the famous Yale backfield known as the "Baby Bulls" and was drafted by the Giants expecting to be the team's new fullback.

"But then they drafted Tucker Frederickson in the same draft and they made him a fullback, too," Mercein said. "Allie and I just got off on the wrong foot. I was disappointed and frustrated."

Nonetheless, Mercein was the Giants' leading rusher in 1966 with 327 yards but his relationship with Sherman continued to deteriorate. As the 1967 season opened, the Giants planned to release Mercein and let him sign elsewhere.

"Then Allie says he wants me back to kick field goals because I'd done a lot of that in college," Mercein said. "I said, 'Allie, I haven't kicked in two years and, besides, I have a pulled groin muscle.' He said, 'I don't care. That's all you're going to do and you miss a kick, you're cut.' It was crazy."

He gained his release from the Giants and was planning to sign with the Washington Redskins on a Monday early in the '67 season.

"But Sunday night the Packers called," he said. "Coach Lombardi took a chance on me. He resurrected a career that had gone off the rails in New York."

The Packers needed help at running back after an injury to starter Jim Grabowski and Lombardi liked Mercein's size and versatility.

He was part of the special teams and saw spot duty as running back, rushing for 56 yards in six games and scoring a touchdown.

And his name may well have been lost to history if not for key back-to-back plays in the game that would come to be known as "The Ice Bowl." And, once again, he found himself in the right place at the right time when Grabowski re-injured his knee in pregame warm-ups and couldn't play. That put Mercein back in the lineup and into history.

"This was our last chance," Mercein recalled of the final drive that started at the Green Bay 32-yard-line with barely four minutes left to play and the Packers trailing 17–14.

Mercein started the five with a 6-yard pass reception and then he gained seven yards on a run.

But the drive seemed to be stalling when both Mercein and halfback Donny Anderson did something remarkable—they spoke up in the huddle.

"You just didn't talk back to Bart [Starr] in the huddle," Mercein said. "But I spoke up and said, 'I'm open in the left flat.' The linebackers weren't focusing on me and I told Bart that I was open if he needed me. Donny said he was open too. It was something we never did but we couldn't hold back. You had to pass the ball to gain any yardage because the field was complete ice."

The very next play Starr indeed found Mercein open in the left flat. He took the short pass and ran 19 yards to the Cowboys' 11-yard line. The next play, Mercein got the ball and roared up the middle for an 8-yard gain to the Cowboys' 3.

"The play worked perfectly," Mercein said.

Three plays later, and with just sixteen seconds remaining in the game, the Packers were perched at the Cowboys' 1 and facing a decision.

Two plays had gained little because the backs couldn't get their footing due to the field. As Starr discussed the final play with Lombardi on the sideline, Mercein was certain the ball would go to him.

Instead, in the famous sideline sequence, Starr suggested a quarterback sneak to Lombardi who responded, "Run it and let's get the hell out of here."

No one on the field knew what was coming, not even Mercein, who saw Starr wedge his way into the end zone. Mercein can be seen in that iconic photo diving over Starr in what many people assumed was a leap of joy. But Mercein said he couldn't stop from the momentum he'd built up and was only showing the officials that he had not helped push into the end zone, which could have resulted in a penalty.

"It was a great call," Mercein said.

The win vaulted the Packers into Super Bowl II against the Oakland Raiders and Mercein, who had started the previous two playoff games, had expected to get the call again for the championship. Instead, Lombardi started Ben Wilson at fullback and Mercein was relegated to backup duty, carrying the ball just once as Green Bay rolled to the easy victory.

That was to be Lombardi's last game as the Packers' head coach and Phil Bengston, Lombardi's longtime defensive coordinator, took over and Lombardi assumed his role as Packers' general manager.

"A nice guy but over his head in that position," Mercein said of Bengston.

Unfortunately for Mercein, who had always been so good at finding himself in the right place at the right time, one night found himself in the wrong place at the wrong time that next season.

He was out with his road roommate, Phil Vandersea, at a Green Bay bar called "My Mother's Place" when all hell broke loose. The wife of another Packers player had stormed the bar with a gun looking for her husband who had sworn he was at a team meeting and not out carousing.

"The police came with lights flashing and Coach showed up, too," Mercein said. "Now we didn't have curfew then so us being at a bar was no big deal but he asked me what I was doing there. I said, 'I'm just having a drink. Can I buy you one?' He didn't like that. The next day he called me into his office and fined me and it was never the same with him."

In the meantime, Mercein had run into Lombardi, who was planning to take over the head coach/general manager duties of the Washington Redskins.

"I ran into him on the golf course and he asked me if I'd like to be his fullback with the Redskins," Mercein said. "I said, 'Of course.'"

With his relationship with Bengston falling, he was placed on waivers in 1969 and planned to join Lombardi in Washington when the coach was struck down with cancer. Lombardi died in the summer of 1970.

Bill Austin took over as head coach and wanted his own players.

"There were several ex-Packers playing for the Redskins under Coach Lombardi and Bill Austin called us all in and released us," Mercein said.

He went to the New York Jets but a foot injury and the lure of a new career were pulling at him.

"But I love the game and I wanted to play," he said.

But he called it a career after 1970 and decided to go into the world of investment banking, which had been calling to him for several years.

"I took my law boards in college and Wall Street was kind of beckoning me," he said. "It was a seamless transition for me."

He would go on to work as a block trader for several Wall Street firms for forty years, only retiring in 2012.

"It's a young man's business," Mercein said. "I've had a very successful career on Wall Street."

But he will never forget his magical year in Green Bay when being in the right place at the right time placed him among the most unexpected of legends of a legendary organization.

"It will always be special to me," he said.

STERLING SHARPE

"Just a really smart guy."

STERLING SHARPE

Position: Wide receiver. Ht: 6'0" Wt: 210

Born: April 6, 1965. Packers career: 1988–94

Career Highlights: *First-round draft pick of the Packers in 1988 out of the University of South Carolina . . . Caught 595 passes, which through 2014 is the second-most in team history . . . His 8,134 receiving yards is third-best in team history . . . Scored 65 touchdowns in just seven seasons . . . Named to Pro Bowl in 1989, 1990, 1992, 1993, 1994 . . . All Pro selection in 1989, 1992, 1993 . . . Led the league in receiving in 1989, 1992, 1993 . . . Inducted into Packers Hall of Fame in 2002 . . . Wore No. 84.*

Perception is often reality, especially in professional sports. Too many athletes have learned the hard way that how you react in public can make the difference between being beloved, tolerated or simply ignored by devoted fans.

Perhaps that's nowhere more in evidence than in Green Bay, where the Packers are first, last, and always in the hearts of fans.

Sterling Sharpe runs a reverse against the Vikings at Lambeau Field on
September 4, 1994. (AP Photo/John Ehlers)

They give their love to players easily and rarely turn on them unless given good reason.

One longtime Packers fan favorite Gilbert Brown understood that early and realized that even on those days you don't feel like being a Packer, you're a Packer anyway.

Case in point is one Sterling Sharpe, who could have had Packers Nation, and indeed the entire state of Wisconsin and much of the upper Midwest, in his hands if he so chose.

But that's not what he wanted or needed.

Charismatic and intelligent, not to mention one of the NFL's best receivers in the late 1980s and early '90s, Sharpe made the conscious choice to do his job the best he could and then go home to South Carolina when the season was done. He met his responsibilities but was never one to mingle with fans or offer a glimpse of who he was and what made him tick.

It was, quite simply, nobody's business.

Criticism his rookie season by local media stung him and for the remainder of his career, he would not speak to state media. And without an outlet to learn who he was or why he did what he did, fans were left with the perception that he was aloof and unfriendly and didn't give a damn.

An incorrect assessment? Maybe. But time and distance has helped reshape the image of Sterling Sharpe in the minds of Packers fans. They know now what he went through just to play every week, especially that final season in 1994 when a controversial holdout was followed by a painful toe injury and concluded with a shocking retirement brought on by yet another injury.

And now fans wonder what might have been had Sharpe stayed healthy and kept playing.

What would the combination of Sharpe and quarterback Brett Favre have accomplished had they had more time together?

What kind of numbers would he have put up? Where would the Packers, who still reached back-to-back Super Bowls in 1996–97, have gone if Sharpe had still been playing?

Now Sharpe is recalled as a great receiver, perhaps a bit misunderstood, who was inducted into the Packers Hall of Fame and, in the minds of many NFL observers, should be in the Pro Football Hall of Fame.

He caught 595 passes for 8,134 yards and 65 touchdowns in his seven seasons. He held the league record for most receptions in a season, 108 in 1992, and was a five-time Pro Bowler and a three-time All Pro selection.

There was also a side to Sharpe that he kept hidden—perhaps on purpose and, just maybe, because he wasn't sure how to make it public.

Former Packers running back Darrell Thompson learned a love of football that he wasn't sure he'd ever find again after watching Sharpe and how he approached the game. And while Sharpe did develop a reputation among Packers fans as being standoffish and, frankly, rude, Thompson saw something different.

He talked about Sharpe's insistence on answering every fan letter he received personally.

"Every Tuesday [the players' off day], he'd be in the locker room with this stack of mail," Thompson said. "I know, because I was there too. Of course, his stack was bigger than mine. But he sat there and answered every one of them, signed every autograph. He did whatever he could."

Thompson also saw what a competitor Sharpe was on the field. Sharpe's arguments with Favre, and their approach to the game, are well known now. Sharpe was more laid-back while Favre was fiery, and the two often clashed.

But back then, Thompson saw in Sharpe a guy who was devoted to playing the game the right way.

"He was also the smartest person I have ever played with," Thompson said.

He recalled a game in 1993 when the young Favre called a play in the huddle at the end of the game.

"So Brett calls a play and Sterling tells him you can't run that because the right personnel isn't in the game," Thompson said. "So Brett calls another one and Sterling said, 'No, you can't run that either.' The third time, he calls a play and Sterling says, 'Yeah, we can do that.' Just a really smart guy."

Sharpe joined a Packers team that was struggling for its identity in 1988. He was the first draft pick of new head coach Lindy Infante and he did little to disappoint, catching 55 passes.

But he did drop a number of passes that season as well and when it was pointed out to him in the media, he decided at that point he had nothing more to say to local reporters, and he maintained that stance throughout his career.

It was unfortunate because Sharpe developed into one of the league's best receivers, growing sure-handed and fearless over the middle and willing to deal out as much punishment as he received.

His reputation would grow throughout the league under Infante, but he would find a new level of productivity when Mike Holmgren became head coach in 1992.

Always the focal point of the offense, Holmgren's offense brought him even more into the process, and with Favre delivering the ball, the two became a devastating combination.

In 1992, he set league records with 108 receptions and 1,461 yards. He also scored 13 touchdowns. But in typical Sharpe fashion, the day he set the record, in a season finale loss to the

Minnesota Vikings that eliminated the Packers from playoff contention, he was nowhere to be found afterward, refusing to speak about the game, the record or anything else.

One reporter even threatened to wait in Sharpe's locker until he showed up. Neither, of course, happened.

He set another record the next season with 112 receptions for 1,274 yards and 11 scores.

But the punishment was already taking a toll. And in 1994, as the Packers were primed to make their run toward the league's upper echelon, Sharpe took a step that he viewed as necessary but everyone else, including most of his teammates, saw as selfish.

Just a day before the season opener at Lambeau Field against the Vikings, Sharpe threatened to sit out the game unless his contract was renegotiated. The timing enraged Holmgren and Favre, especially, who saw it as a selfish power play that could not have come at a worse time.

Given assurances the contract dispute would be addressed, Sharpe agreed to play and, for the first time, he was exposed to widespread booing by Packers fans. But in typical fashion, he put perceptions behind him, caught seven passes for 53 yards and scored a touchdown as the Packers posted a crucial win.

But it would never be quite the same between Sharpe and his teammates even as Sharpe put up Herculean numbers while playing through a severely injured toe that wouldn't allow him to practice most of the season.

He ended up catching 94 passes for 1,119 yards and a staggering 18 touchdowns, including four against the Dallas Cowboys in a Thanksgiving Day game played before a national TV audience.

The beginning of the end came for Sharpe in a December 18, 1994 game against the Atlanta Falcons in Milwaukee. On a seemingly innocuous second quarter block of Falcons' cornerback Brad Edwards, Sharpe fell back on his stomach, writhing in pain.

He experienced numbness in his arms and did not play the rest of the game. He was cleared to play in the season finale the next week in Tampa, but when he was tackled in the fourth quarter, the numbness returned.

More testing revealed a stunning diagnosis: Sharpe had a narrowing of his spinal column that had been there his entire life but had never been noticed on any exams before.

He was ruled out for the Packers postseason run and underwent vertebrae fusion surgery in hopes of saving his career. When Sharpe refused to take a pay cut after surgery, which caused him to miss the entire 1995 season, the Packers released him.

Sharpe filed suit against the Packers seeking to get his $3.2 million salary, but it was dismissed.

Sharpe considered returning to play but never hooked on with another NFL team. And, in a stroke of irony, he started a career as an analyst, first for ESPN and later with the NFL Network, where he's part of the "NFL Playbook" segment. The media, for which he'd had no use for years, was now employing him.

All is forgiven now between Sharpe and Packers fans, who have learned that what you did sometimes matters more than how you did it. And sometimes, that's enough.

BRETT FAVRE

"I always wanted to play."

BRETT FAVRE

Position: Quarterback. Ht: 6'2" Wt: 220

Born: October 10, 1969. Packers career: 1992–2007.

Career Highlights: Third-round draft pick of the Atlanta Falcons in 1991 out of the University of Southern Mississippi . . . Traded to Packers for a first-round draft pick in 1992 . . . Packers all-time leader in touchdown passes (442), passing yardage (8,754), interceptions (286) and a dozen other passing records . . . Three NFL MVP awards (1995–96–97) . . . Still holds NFL record for most consecutive starts (321 including playoffs) . . . Led NFL four times in touchdown passes (1995–96–97–2003) . . . Member of the NFL's 1990s All Decade Team . . . Inducted into Green Bay Packers Hall of Fame . . . Wore No. 4.

B rett Favre is at peace these days. From his compound deep in his beloved Mississippi woods, he is finally able to look back on a twenty-year NFL career that, in many ways, still defies explanation.

Brett Favre and John Elway prior to Super Bowl XXXII. (AP Photo/
Dave Martin)

Who was he? A great quarterback who probably should have been even greater? The NFL's longtime leader in touchdown passes who is also the NFL's all-time leader in interceptions? An ironman who played an astounding and likely never to be seen again 321 consecutive games yet never knew when it was time to walk away? A devoted family man who was given to bizarre lapses in judgment? One of the greatest Packers in history but whose relationship with fans is still undergoing repair?

He is all those things and more.

"Great teammate, a great guy," said Packers running back Dorsey Levens who played with Favre during the years when he was the game's best quarterback and the Packers were the best team in the NFC. "People forget what a great competitor he was. He was a practical jokester and even though he was a three-time league MVP, he was always able to be himself. He was just a good old country boy and that's really who he was."

The rebuilding of the Brett Favre image has been ongoing since he finally retired, again and for good, after the 2010 season.

It had been a difficult season for Favre who, the season before, seemed rejuvenated. That 2009 season, his first with the Vikings that brought fury from most Packers fans, he had thrown for 4,200 yards and 33 touchdowns, his highest total since 1997. More amazing, he only threw seven interceptions, by far the fewest he'd ever thrown, and seemed to have, once again, cheated time.

Favre played so well, he probably should have won his fourth league MVP award. But he was content to take a second team to the Super Bowl and his Vikings seemed poised to do just that in the NFC title game when he reverted to an old pattern and threw a costly interception in overtime, leading to a loss to the New Orleans Saints.

He could not repeat that magic in 2010 and a difficult season only got worse on December 13, 2010, when Favre's consecutive game streak, which had started in September 1992, ended due to a shoulder injury.

The next week, he returned only to be knocked unconscious on the frozen field of the University of Minnesota football stadium against the Chicago Bears.

The injuries—too numerous to mention and which had plagued him for years—finally beat the forty-one-year-old down and he realized it was time to walk away. After two "retirements" and hinting at several others, it was finally a reality for a player that the NFL won't see again for a long time.

And even he knew it this time.

"The stress to be good week in and week out," Favre told the *Milwaukee Journal Sentinel's* Tyler Dunne. "The expectations I had placed on myself, not to mention the expectations everyone else had, were just too great. There was no way I could surpass it. And no matter how good I played, the next week I had to be better. And that's the mentality that drives you. But also, it drove me bananas. When you lost, it stuck with you and still sticks with me forever. I'll think about a loss rather than the fifteen great wins."

It's a far cry from the unruly, undisciplined kid who entered the league in 1991 and was not-so-affectionately nicknamed "the Pillsbury Doughboy" by Atlanta Falcons' coach Jerry Glanville, who never knew what to do with him.

To Glanville, Favre was an overweight, screw-up party boy who would only see playing time, in Glanville's words, if every other quarterback on the roster was in a car accident.

Favre did play in one game and had his first pass intercepted and returned for a touchdown.

But new Green Bay Packers general manager Ron Wolf saw something special in Favre, a player he scouted the year before when he was working for the New York Jets. And had the Falcons not selected him in the third round that year, Wolf would have.

It was a year later now and Wolf had another chance to grab the quarterback he thought could be truly special. So Wolf dealt Green Bay's first-round draft pick in 1992 to Atlanta for Favre, providing new head coach, Mike Holmgren, with a young, talented quarterback he could develop.

If the quarterback would listen, that is.

It is now part of Packers' legend that Favre would step in as the starter in the third week of the season after starter Don Majkowski went down with an ankle injury. Favre would go on to lead the Packers to a last-second win over the befuddled Cincinnati Bengals as Favre called plays and formations that didn't even exist yet somehow made it all work.

The legend of Favre had taken root.

Over the next fifteen years, he would direct the Packers to two Super Bowls, winning one and losing the other, as well as establishing himself as a force of nature in the NFL.

He could just as easily throw five interceptions in a game as he could throw five touchdowns. He would defiantly and confidently pass into triple coverage, certain he could throw through a defender. He could make the easy plays seem difficult and the impossible plays seem routine.

That was Favre, and fans, teammates, and opponents grew to expect it.

But he also established himself as one of the toughest players in the league. He would suffer shoulder, elbow, thumb and ankle injuries and play through them as well as shaking off concussions and the kind of violent hits that at times would make him cough up blood.

"He had an air of cockiness about him," Levens said. "He wouldn't back down from anybody. I remember he always had these great battles with [Tampa Bay Buccaneers defensive tackle] Warren Sapp. One time Warren hit him so hard and Brett popped up and got in his face said, 'I'm going to be here all day.' Then Brett came back to the huddle and when no one could see him he kind of bent over and said, 'Man, he hit me hard.'"

But Favre believed that was the only way to play.

"I always wanted to play and I always expected to play," he said.

One game in 1995, he could barely walk on a severely sprained ankle yet still threw five touchdowns to beat the Chicago Bears. In 2003, he shook off a broken thumb and threw two touchdowns in a crucial NFC Central win over the Vikings at his personal house of horrors, the Metrodome.

"People said I was crazy to play in that game," he said. "They said you can sit this one out and not catch any grief over it. But I really wanted to play and redeem myself."

And in perhaps his greatest performance under crushing circumstances, later that same season Favre threw for 399 yards and four touchdowns in a Monday night rout of the Oakland Raiders two days after his beloved father died.

"I knew he would have wanted me to play," Favre said simply.

In his sixteen seasons as Green Bay's quarterback, the Packers suffered just one losing season and he directed them to five NFC championship games.

But his last years in Green Bay were fraught with uncertainty and controversy.

He began entertaining ideas of retirement toward the end of the 2006 season, teasing fans and media all offseason about his future. But he returned for 2007 and played well, throwing for 4,155 yards and 28 touchdowns as the Packers went 13–3. But in the NFC title game, he threw an ill-advised overtime interception and Green Bay lost to the New York Giants.

It would be his last game as a Green Bay Packer, though no one really knew it at the time.

He hinted again at retirement that offseason and then in March 2008, the bombshell came.

In a tearful press conference, Favre announced he was quitting, saying, "I know can play, I just don't think I want to."

The Packers prepared to move on with backup Aaron Rodgers until Favre announced a few months later that he had been premature in his retirement announcement. He still wanted to play and he wanted his starting job back with the Packers.

But general manager Ted Thompson and head coach Mike McCarthy had settled on Rodgers and agreed to bring Favre back in a backup role. He refused.

The collision between Favre and the organization split Packers fans, half of whom wanted Favre back and the other half furious he would manipulate the team like that.

Eventually, after negotiations between Favre and the team, he was traded to the New York Jets for a fourth-round draft pick.

Favre played one season with the Jets before again announcing his retirement.

But he was lured back out again by the Vikings, a decision that enraged Packers fans. He could play if he wanted, but going to the archrival Vikings? That was the last straw.

When Favre returned to Green Bay for a 2010 game against the Packers, Lambeau Field erupted in boos and vitriol and all Favre did was play superbly, throwing for 244 yards and four touchdowns, and beating the Packers for the second time that season.

It was at once a thrilling and sad moment for Favre, who had made Green Bay his home for years and was now treated as the enemy.

A little more than a year later, beaten up and tired, he finally walked away, though several teams did try to lure him back. This time, he said no.

Yet, even today, Favre believes with a little work, he could have his arm back in shape to throw at the NFL level. But he knows he has nothing left to prove.

He told Dunne with a laugh that he might return if he could get guarantees from defensive players that no one would hit him.

Since his retirement, Favre has settled into the life of something akin to an antebellum southern gentleman—but with a tractor.

He still lives near his hometown of Kiln, Mississippi, but now owns more than 400 acres with a self-contained nature preserve where he can hunt to his heart's content.

He works the land and endorses a number of products from beard and nose hair trimmers to lawn and garden equipment to jeans. And he still finds himself in demand for endorsements, earning a reported $3 million a year as of 2015.

He has been asked to do TV work and has done it sparingly, even though it's not what he does best or what he even likes to do.

He also has a number of projects he works on, including a sports social media network called Sqor.com. But he admits he's no digital expert.

He also took pleasure in serving as offensive coordinator for his alma mater, Oak Grove High School, helping lead it to the Mississippi state championship.

He has no desire to be a coach at any level above high school because, as he's said often, no one should learn the game the way he played it.

The rehabbing of Favre's image continues. He was to be inducted into the Packers Hall of Fame and have his No. 4 retired during the 2014 season, and was going to appear with another Packers' icon, Bart Starr. But Starr suffered a stroke and heart attack and plans were postponed.

Favre's No. 4 jersey still sits in a Lambeau Field room, framed and ready to go for the day he's accepted back into the family.

It's a moment for which he's waited a long time and which he knows will bring him back to the place he always belonged.

"I'm a Packer and I'll always be a Packer," he said.